California Natur

INTRODUCTION
TO THE

NATURAL HISTORY

OF

SOUTHERN CALIFORNIA

BY
EDMUND C. JAEGER
AND
ARTHUR C. SMITH

ILLUSTRATIONS BY GENE M. CHRISTMAN

UNIVERSITY OF CALIFORNIA PRESS

BERKELEY, LOS ANGELES, LONDON   1971

UNIVERSITY OF CALIFORNIA PRESS
BERKELEY AND LOS ANGELES
UNIVERSITY OF CALIFORNIA PRESS, LTD.
LONDON, ENGLAND
© 1966 BY THE REGENTS OF THE UNIVERSITY OF CALIFORNIA
SECOND PRINTING, 1971
ISBN: 0-520-00601-1
LIBRARY OF CONGRESS CATALOG NUMBER 65-27936
PRINTED IN THE UNITED STATES OF AMERICA

CONTENTS

NOTE ON ILLUSTRATIONS: the cover shows (moving clockwise) gulls at the shore, the Desert Big Horn Sheep, Ocotillo, and the One-Leaf Piñon Pine. The illustration on p. 4 shows cormorants and the Torrey Pine. The kodachrome of Catalina Island was taken by E. Yale Dawson.

INTRODUCTION

By nature man is a creature of curiosity. Especially is this true in childhood. If this curiosity, the continual desire to name and to know the nature of things, is allowed to develop freely, and satisfaction is found in gaining further knowledge, this seeking spirit is more alive than ever when adulthood comes.

The purpose of this series of Southern California Natural History Guides is to help us organize our thinking about birds, common and uncommon weeds, the flowers of the field, the trees of streamside and mountain. Many kinds of insects and spiders will be named, the mammals and reptiles identified, as well as the strange and beautiful creatures of the sea, and their habits described. It is hoped that many will be stimulated to make original discoveries and thus add to our scientific knowledge.

With your Southern California Natural History Guides in hand, you will wish to explore the beaches, the mountains, and the desert, even your backyard garden and the neighboring vacant lots and fields. Through such excursions you become self-entertaining and do not need to spend money to hire others to entertain you. The money thus saved can be spent on books and film for your camera or for travel to far places.

It has been truly said that you know only the ground over which you have walked. The automobile is most useful when it takes us to new and otherwise inaccessible places where we may get out and *walk,* take time to listen to the entrancing sounds of the outdoor world, and let the creatures of nature move about us without fear. Then we use our noses as aesthetic organs to bring to us the woodsy odors of the forest or the tangy smells of sagebrush and creosote bush. It is good to watch the slow-moving and colorful creatures of the tidepools or the graceful flight of sea birds. As we roam the earth on foot, we become intimately acquainted with rocks and minerals, note the varied forms of the land and the contrasting colors of moving clouds against a background of the bright blue heaven. At night we appreciate anew the majesty of the many-starred sky.

Because the southern California guides are well illustrated with photographs, drawings, and charts, you will be able to identify and name many heretofore unfamiliar things. It is better to know the scientific name of an animal, plant, or rock, for it is more exact than the common name and is the one used by people the world over. After all, scientific names cast in Latin form are little more difficult to remember than common names if we know their origin and literal meanings and use them often enough.

This first volume of the *Southern California Natural History Guide Series* provides an introduction to the large and diversified southern California region, its physical features, climate, and seasons. Following this are informative statements on plants and animals and their interrelationships. A special section deals with biotic communities, tells where characteristic plants and animals may be found, and suggests field trips to acquaint the seeker with living things in their natural environments. Museums and organizations concerned with natural history and the conservation of natural resources are listed, along with references to books, journals, and magazines which will be helpful in further study.

PHYSICAL DESCRIPTION

The name southern California is arbitrarily used here to designate the arid parts of the state from San Luis Obispo County southward to the Mexican border and eastward to Death Valley and the Colorado River. The southernmost Sierra Nevada is not included. Other volumes of this series may vary in the exact geographic area covered.

Southern California comprises oceanic islands, sea-shore, coastal plains, great inland valleys, and internally drained basins with east-west and north-south dissected mountain ranges between. There are many low hills, some isolated, others seemingly buttressing the mountains. The northward islands owe their existence to subsidence of the western end of the east-west directed Santa Monica Mountains.

Between the mountains and the sea, the coastal plain varies from rather wide to narrow, sometimes extending inland and cut across by a few small streams, such as the Santa Inez, Santa Clara, Ventura, Los Angeles, Santa Ana, and San Luis Rey rivers. Most of the larger valleys and some of the upland slopes are devoted to argriculture and urban development

Much of San Diego County, except for a rather narrow strip of marine terraces and geologically young mesa lands along the ocean, consists of chaparral- and oak-covered hills and mountains dissected and entrenched by dendritic arroyos, sometimes containing small streams, many of them dry in summer. These brush-covered hills and mountains, rising higher and higher toward the east, culminate in elevated areas where scattered forests of live and decidous oaks, Incense Cedar, Yellow Pine, Sugar Pine, and other coniferous trees grow. Mount Palomar is 6,158 feet high; Cuyamaca Mountain, with an elevation of 6,515 feet, is the highest point in the county. This part of the Peninsular Province mountain mass is still being uplifted. The Palomar, Vulcan, and Laguna mountains are thought to be upraised fault blocks.

The mountains comprising the east-west trending Transverse Ranges are the Santa Inez, Santa Monica, San Gabriel, San Bernardino, and Little San Bernardino mountains. Southward from these are the north-south oriented Peninsular Mountains made up of the San Jacinto, Santa Rosa, Laguna, Vallecito, and outlying detached Santa Ana mountains. The Peninsular Mountains extending southward make up the backbone of the peninsula of Baja California.

North of the Transverse Ranges lies the vast arid Mojave Desert, and east of the Peninsular Ranges is the barren Colorado Desert of lower elevations, a depressed block of the earth's surface characterized by deep alluvial soils, old beach lines, and salt deposits of ancient Lake Cahuilla.

The Mojave Desert is dominated by many north- and south-dissected hills and low mountains between which are broad basins having no drainage outlet to the sea. Excess storm waters flowing into them cause the formation of clay- or salt-surfaced dry lakes or "salt pans," which may be covered at times by shallow sheets of water.

The Colorado Desert trough contains the present below-sea-level Salton Sea. Its ancestral waters may once have been connected with the Gulf of California. The area is now isolated from the sea by a low bar of silt at the mouth of the Colorado River. The lowest parts of the Salton depression have several times been temporarily filled with fresh water from the river, the last time in 1905 and 1906. The dissolving of accumulated salts on its ancient floor has made this recently-formed inland body of water almost as salty as the sea. Owing to evaporation and the addition of new salts carried by irrigation and drainage waters from the surrounding hills and mountains, its salt content is gradually increasing; perhaps by the year 2000 it will be too salty to support any kind of fish life.

The Colorado River forming the southeast boundary of California has in ages past brought down and deposited vast amounts of silt, which now form the rich soils of the agricultural lands of the Palo Verde and Imperial Valleys and the Yuma Plains.

The evidence and effects of past earth movements on a vast scale are apparent in southern California. Aerial photography shows many minor and several major earth fractures or faults. Slippage along these lines of weakness continually occurs. The long, deeply-penetrating San Andreas Fault cuts through the region from northwest to southeast. This longest and best-defined fault runs through the northern parts of the San Gabriel Mountains, along the southern base of the San Bernardino Mountains, and through the Coachella Valley. Earth movement along this great fissure, rivaled only by the Rift Valley Fault of Africa, is mainly horizontal.

Other major faults are the Owens Valley, Tejon, Garlock, San Jacinto, Elsinore, Long Beach, San Gabriel, and Santa Inez. Recent movements of considerable intensity have taken place along most of these fracture zones: Owens Valley (1872), San Jacinto (1899 and 1918), Santa Barbara (1925), Long Beach (1933), Imperial Valley (1940), Arvin-Tehachapi (1952).

Volcanic activity, some of it fairly recent, is unusually evident in the desert region, where, as at Amboy and in Owens Valley, basaltic lava flows and well-formed, little-weathered cinder cones are seen.

Stratified sedimentary rocks, some of them fossil-bearing, dominate the plains and mountains near the Pacific Ocean. Isolated masses of limestone occur inland at such places as Tehachapi, Crestmore, Victor-

The Major Faults
in Southern California

GMC

ville, along the north base of the San Bernardino Mountains, Clark Mountain, Kingston Mountain, and Ivanpah Mountain. Limestone may be of organic or inorganic origin.

Granitic and granitoid rocks, often much altered, form the greater mass of the San Gabriel, San Bernardino, Little San Bernardino, Santa Rosa, and Laguna mountains.

Death Valley is a large, unique, and colorful depressed portion of the earth's crust in the northeastern Mojave Desert. It is bounded by high, upraised, tilted fault-block mountains, the Panamint and Cottonwood mountains on the west and the Black, Funeral, and Grapevine mountains on the east. A large lake formerly filled the basin. Among the more spectacular of its scenic features are great aprons of alluvial materials which streams have brought out of the deep, narrow canyons. At a point in the valley called Badwater is the lowest spot (282 ft. below sea level) in the United

States. Only a few miles to the west, in the Sierra Nevada, is the highest point (Mount Whitney, 14,495 ft.) in the continental United States outside Alaska.

Most of southern California's streams are intermittent, flowing to the sea only during heavy rains and soon thereafter. We call some of the larger ones "rivers," which seems strange to Midwesterners and Easterners, who have a very different concept of rivers. Streams carrying the largest amounts of water are the Santa Inez, Santa Clara, Ventura, Los Angeles, San Gabriel, Santa Ana, San Luis Rey, and Mojave rivers. Some mountain streams flow throughout the year; however, most of them end near their point of debouching at or near the lower end of the canyons in which they flow. Their waters then either sink into coarse gravels and sands or are led off in man-made drains to irrigate fields and orchards or to supply urban communities.

The Mojave River is a classic example of an "upside-down" stream, for its waters flow beneath its sandy bed instead of on the surface. The Amargosa River of the Death Valley region, highly charged with minerals, hence called "the river of bitter waters," is another "upside-down" river. The Mojave River at times of fullest flow discharges into Cronese Dry Lake or Soda Lake, the latter sometimes called the "sink of the Mojave." The Amargosa River flows into Death Valley.

There are only a few natural freshwater lakes in the region, but in several places the waters have been impounded behind artificial dams. Some of these, especially along the southeastern boundary of the state, are of considerable size. Lake Havasu, Imperial Lake, and Laguna Lake are kept filled by the constantly flowing Colorado River, which arises in the Rocky Mountains of Colorado and has numerous feeder streams in Utah and Nevada.

CLIMATE

The evidence suggests that, before 8000 B.C., wetter climates prevailed in southern California. Since then the climate has been much as it is today, with wet and dry periods of a decade or two, alternating in irregular fashion. We now have a subtropical or, more specifically, Mediterranean type of climate, characterized by mild winters, warm springs and autumns, and, except along the coast and in the high mountains, hot, dry summers; the summer daytime temperatures are especially high in desert areas. Morning fogs frequently cool the coastal plains, and at times may reach inland to the mountain borders.

Rains usually occur in late autumn, winter, and early spring. Occasional summer rain-bearing clouds are brought in with storms which originate in the southwest Pacific, the Gulf of California, or even the Gulf of Mexico, and sweep across the land northward and northwestward. Most of the tropical storms which reach southern California are tail ends of storms of great intensity, known in Baja California and western Mexico as *chubascos*.

The prevailing winds of cismontane southern California are landward from the west and northwest. Winter rain-bearing winds are from the southwest and west. In late autumn and winter, strong dry north winds (in some places east winds), known as Santa Anas, blow across the coastal valleys (usually following rains) for periods of three to five days. Owing to compressional (adiabatic) heating, they are generally warm enough to prevent frost formation, and hence are a great boon to vegetable growers and orchardists.

[13]

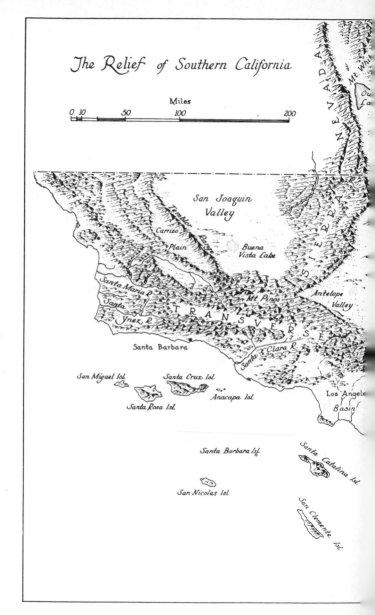

The Relief of Southern California

Miles
0 10   50   100   200

San Joaquin Valley

Carrizo

Plain

Buena Vista Lake

Santa Maria R.

Santa

Ynez R.

TRANSVERSE

Mt Pinos

Antelope Valley

Santa Barbara

Santa Clara R.

San Miguel Isl.

Santa Cruz Isl.

Anacapa Isl.

Los Angeles

Basin

Santa Rosa Isl.

Santa Barbara Isl.

Santa Catalina Isl.

San Nicolas Isl.

San Clemente Isl.

SIERRA NEVADA

Mt. Whit

N

NEVADA

Death Valley

Panamint Range

Amargosa Range

Searles Lake

MOJAVE DESERT

Mojave River

Needles

San Antonio

Cajon Pass

ANGELES

Big Bear Lake

River

Mt. San Gorgonio

Mt. San Jacinto

PENINSULAR

COLORADO

Salton Sea

Mt. Palomar

San Luis Rey R.

Imperial Valley

Diego

Mt Laguna

ARIZONA

COLORADO DESERT

Colorado River

RANGE

Sierra de Juarez

Laguna Salada ó Macuata

Gene M. Christman

When inland high-pressure areas build up over the deserts in summer, especially in June, late August, and September, uncomfortably high temperatures may occur in normally cool coastal regions. It may then actually be cooler at Barstow and Palm Springs on the desert than at Los Angeles, Santa Ana, and San Diego. As the already warm desert air moves southward and westward and descends through the mountain passes, it heats up at the rate of about 5½°F. for every 1,000 feet it drops. It is a Santa Ana type of condition, but without the usual strong and gusty winds that occur in late fall and winter northers.

On the average summer day a rather brisk marine onshore breeze sweeps inland, beginning at 9 to 10:30 in the morning, greatly modifying the atmospheric temperature from the seacoast to the mountains.

Southern California's summers are markedly fair (cloudless) and calm. In interior areas of low elevation (1,500 ft. to 3,000 ft.) the daytime highs may reach 100° to 112° F., but in the mountains above 5,000 feet the thermometer seldom registers above 90° F., often not over 80° or 85° F. Regardless of high daytime maxima, the nights are usually cool enough so that even on the high desert comfortable sleep is possible. The winter weather is far more variable, and windier clouded skies with rain (in the mountains snow), are then often experienced.

Because of varied topography and our relation to the cool to cold Pacific Ocean on the west, and the vast high Great Basin deserts on the north, there may be many degrees of difference in temperature at places of close proximity both in winter and in summer.

When heavy spring and summer fogs occur on the coastal plains and cismontane valleys, winds of great intensity (25 to 50 miles per hour) sweep across the deserts, blowing clouds of dust and sand before them. Then visibility may be reduced to nearly zero, and highways may be closed to traffic from several hours to a day.

Snow falls infrequently, usually between early November and April. When it rains in the valleys, the mountains may be covered with snow even down to the 2,000-foot level. Snow may fall on the Mojave Desert several times in a winter, but seldom does it cover the coastal plains, almost never the lowlands of the warmer Colorado Desert. In midwinter snow has been seen as near the coast as San Diego. Melting is rapid; these lowland snows seldom remain more than a few hours. Snow in the mountains may remain for several months.

The average annual precipitation in the coastal areas varies from 18 inches at Santa Barbara to about 11 inches in Riverside and San Diego. In desert areas the maxima may be as low as 2 inches and seldom more than 8 or 9 inches. Furnace Creek Ranch in Death Valley receives under 2 inches, El Centro less than 3 inches a year. The mountain areas may receive as much as 45 to 50 inches a year (the typical annual totals for the Lake Arrowhead region).

When winter storms approach the southern California coast, southeasterly or southwesterly wind may bring increasing cloudiness. As the warm front approaches, rain begins to fall. The warm front involves the active flow of warm air up over a gently inclined wedge of cold air. The warm air above is cooled by expansion, with resulting cloud formation and rain. Such warm-front rains often last twenty-four hours or longer. They are typically our most effective rains, for they come as steady drizzles, making possible slow absorption of water into the soil, with runoff reduced to a minimum. The cold front follows closely behind the warm-front rains, and consists of a steeply inclined mass of cold air forcing upward the warmer air mass. Rains associated with the cold front are typically of smaller areal extent and duration, although of much greater intensity than the warm-front rains. Although the northern edge of a storm may receive continuous precipitation throughout the storm's duration, the largest part of the area covered by the storm under-goes partial clearing after the passage of the warm-front and before the arrival of the cold-front precipitation. As the cold front passes, the wind shifts to the west and north west. Then, as the front moves east-ward, the skies begin to clear, but cumulus clouds may persist over the mountains for a day or so. Strong, gusty north winds may follow and persist for several days.

The normal growing season for crops varies from 365 days in a year in the low desert regions to less than 120 days in the mountains. Frosts that kill tender plants occur infrequently in the below-sea-level Coachella and Imperial valleys, but on the high Mojave Desert they can be expected every year in winter. Low temperatures (18° to 22° F.) in late No-vember to late February may cause loss of fruit crops and tender vegetables almost anywhere in coastal areas. Temperatures, sometimes as low as 19° F., occur every few years in the vegetable-growing areas of the Imperial and Coachella valleys.

In recent years atmospheric pollution has become a major concern. Over much of southern California, smog caused by automobile, factory, and other wastes occurs almost daily. Clean healthful air is evidently to be enjoyed only on high mountain tops and far inland deserts. The Los Angeles Basin suffers the most. A temperature inversion acts as a lid to hold in the pollutants, and only an occasional cyclonic storm clears the atmosphere. Smogs of eye-smarting proportion are most frequent in late summer and autumn.

(*Suggestion:* Send $1.00 to the Superintendent of Documents, Government Printing Office, Washington, D. C., and get the *Weather Science Study Kit* to help you learn the rudiments of meteorology: It consists of sixteen publications designed to assist persons interested in the weather.)

THE SEASONS

Winter in the lowlands of southern California is very mild by eastern and northern United States standards. Except in the mountains there is little or no snow, and hard frosts are far from common.

Nature's activities are at a low ebb in winter, for cool days and colder nights have brought most plants and many animals to a period of comparative rest. Decidous trees and shrubs lose their leaves, and some animals (most lizards and snakes, some ground squirrels, etc.) become torpid or hibernate. But winter does not mean an end of all nature's activities in southern California, especially in the lowlands of cismontaine valleys and desert basins. November rains induce many plants to begin growth, and such plants as the Desert Sunflower *(Garrea canescens)* and Sand Verbena *(Arbonia villosa aurita)* may already be in bloom in early February. February and March, last of the winter months, are looked upon by many native Californians as the first of spring, especially on the warmer deserts, where the best wildflowers may then appear in abundance. The House Finch, the Roadrunner, Say's Phoebe, and Verdin will now be building nests. The larvae of the sphinx moth are already aboard devouring wildflowers as they prepare for pupation. Winter is a good time to learn to identify the land birds, for those which are here as permanent or winter residents are comparatively few and easy to see. In the lowland areas are Brewer's Blackbird, the Scrub Jay, the Brown Towhee, the White-crowned Sparrow recently arrived from the north, the Red-tailed Hawk and the Sparrow Hawk, and in the mountains the Mountain Chickadee, the Acorn Woodpecker, Steller's Jay, and others. Some owls will be nesting.

Churning ocean waves and high tides cast up many strange shells upon the beaches. The winter rains, if adequate, start wild grasses and annual flowering plants growing and before the season is over you may see, blooming in coastal areas, wild peony, yellow violets, wild mustard, lupines, larkspurs, and shooting stars.

Spring comes early in southern California hills and lowlands. Shrubs now begin to send out new leaves and stems, and before May ends many will have bloomed profusely and set fruit; the wild lilacs *(Ceanothus)* color the foothills with white and dainty blues. The multitude of flowering annuals bloom and set seed. California Poppies, Sun Cups, Tidytips, and larkspurs brighten the flats and foothills of the cismontane valleys. The yellow violets and the wild peony bloom in the shelter of chaparral shrubs.

The season of Colorado Desert flowers is nearly over, but the higher Mojave Desert now begins to display its floral offering of Cassia, Snake's Head, Squaw Cabbage, and numerous yellow composites. In the higher desert mountains, spring flowers continue to bloom until late in May.

In June we expect to see the beginning of the mountain flower show. Lupines, many kinds of Astragalus, Gilia, streamside Lemon Lily, and Wild Forget-me-not reflect the brightness of the summer skies. This is the season of greatest joy for student botanists, who will now be taking to fields and hills to see the colorful "spring" flower show. A host of migratory birds are on their way to their northern breeding grounds. House Finches and blackbirds arrive in flocks, build nests, lay eggs, and raise their young. Vibrant bird songs greet the ear, lizards and snakes resume their activities, and butterflies and moths are on the wing; bees and wasps, large and small, are visiting the nectaries of flowers.

[20]

Summer days are full of life. In the foothill chaparral belt, the dark green of the shrubs begins to change to brown, and the white crepe-petalled Matilija Poppy blooms on long stems in the canyons, especially on northern slopes. In July the scarlet-stemmed Snow Plant, as well as the Bitter Root and species of Pedicularis, may emerge in the pine forests. The clear sunny days are warm enough to call out the cicadas to give their penetrating shrill clatter, to cause chrysalids to release their butterflies. Now comes the chance to learn the food plants of caterpillars, watch them grow and hide as pupae in the soil or among dead leaves. Summer brings a golden opportunity to collect insects at night, using "black light" to attract rare moths and night-flying beetles. Toward the end of summer the Acorn Woodpecker begins to drill holes in pine bark for the storage of acorns; chipmunks and squirrels are laying up their winter stores.

Autumn is the best of all seasons. Bright skies and calm weather invite us to go camping in the lower mountains and on the sandy washes of the desert. Death Valley and the Mojave and Colorado deserts now offer their best to us. The mountains' deciduous trees (California Black Oak, Big-Leaf Maple, etc.)

turn color and drop their leaves. The crisp nights invite the making of small campfires. One can take long walks in the sunshine or seek occasional rests beside smoke trees or creosote bushes while reading such interesting books as Mary Austin's *Land of Little Rain*, Thoreau's *Walden*, or John Muir's *Mountains of California*.

The final months of the year are not without color. The first frosts in the mountains in late September and early October bring hues of yellow and red to the leaves of dogwoods, California Black Oak, cottonwood, willows, Sycamore, and Bracken. Rabbit Brush *(Chrysothamnus)* is now at the height of flowering, and many a roadside and field of deserts and mountains is golden with the flowers of this hardy shrub. Many of the birds that summered in the high mountains to the north take a short rest with us before completing their long migration southward to their winter homes in Central and South America.

In October's bright blue skies we see spectacular gyrations of flocks of the Turkey Vulture preparing for flight to Mexico. Piñon Jays, in great flocks, harvest the nuts of the Piñon Pine in late September and early October.

October is also the month when the California Buck Moth is in flight. This attractive black-and-white moth is a day flyer and can be found near willows and cottonwoods.

THE PLANT WORLD

The good naturalist has unbounded interest in both living and nonliving things—plants, animals, rocks, minerals, and non-living phenomena—weather, climate, the laws of physics and chemistry. He sees nature as a unity, all its phenomena linked together as parts of a vast whole. He seeks to know the laws of Nature and in reverent attitude tries to understand the plants and animals, how each is dependent on the other and is related to its nonliving environment.

The two great common and essential characteristics of plants and animals are their "urge" and ability to grow, and to reproduce themselves. A crystal may grow, but it cannot reproduce itself; it is not alive.

Plants are basic living things, for they take simple nonliving elements and compounds (water, minerals, and carbon dioxide) and, with the aid of energy supplied by the sun, build them into plant substances and tissues upon which all animals are dependent. Directly or indirectly animals eat the plants and, after breaking them down by digestion into simple elements and compounds, recombine them into complex substances *of their own kind.* Plants may vary in size from tiny bacteria only 1/250,000 of an inch across to the giant eucalyptus *(Eucalypus regnum)* of Australia, 326 feet high, or to the largest California redwood *(Sequoia gigantea)*, 367 feet tall and more than 30 feet in diameter. Between these extremes are numerous kinds of flowering plants, trees and shrubs of our gardens, wildflowers and ferns of fields and canyons, roadside weeds, and the less familiar seaweeds, mushrooms, mosses, and liverworts.

The plant kingdom

It is estimated that there are between 250,000 and 350,000 species of plants. For convenience, botanists have divided them into two major groups:

1. Thallophyta* (thal-*of*-it-a): bacteria, pond scums, seaweeds, molds, fungi.
2. Embryophyta (em-bri-*of*-it-a): mosses, ferns, club-mosses, cone-bearers (pines, etc), flowering plants.

The major plant groups are described below:

DIVISION CHLOROPHYTA—5500 species
Green algae: fresh-water and marine species; include sea lettuce, branched stoneworts, *Volvox*, desmids, *Spirogyra, Ulothrix, Oedogonium*, etc.

DIVISION CYANOPHYTA—1500 species
Blue-green algae: fresh-water and marine species; common on damp soil and on rocks; include *Oscillatoria, Anabaena, Rivularia, Microcystis, Nostoc*, etc.

DIVISION EUGLENOPHYTA—300 species
Euglenoids: mostly fresh-water forms; in polluted waters or on damp soil; include *Euglena.*

DIVISION CHRYSOPHYTA—5000 species
Yellow-green algae, Golden-brown algae and the diatoms: mostly aquatic, some fresh-water forms, others marine; some on damp soil, on rocks and in hot springs; include *Tribonema, Vaucheria, Botrydium, Synura, Uroglenopsis, Tabellaria, Cyclotella,* etc.

DIVISION PYRRHOPHYTA—1000 species
Dinoflagellates: mostly salt-water forms, some in fresh water; include *Gymnodinium, Peridinium, Ceratium, Noctiluca,* etc.

DIVISION PHAEOPHYTA—1500 species
Brown algae: mostly marine forms; include kelps and other familiar seaweeds, *Laminaria, Fucus, Dictyota,* etc.

DIVISION RHODOPHYTA—3000 species
Red algae: mostly marine forms, few in fresh water. Many attached to rocks in intertidal zone; include *Porphyra, Dasya, Polysiphonia,* etc.

DIVISION SCHIZOPHYTA—1600 species
Fission plants: microscopic one-celled forms found in virtually every environment; include bacteria, viruses, actinomycetes, etc.

*Unicellular plants (one-celled algae and bacteria) are sometimes combined with the equivalent group of one-celled animals to form the Protista, a term invented by the German biologist Ernst Haeckel to include all unicellular organisms.

DIVISION MYXOMYCOPHYTA—450 species
Slime molds: motile amoeba-like plants common in decaying vegetable matter; include *Cerateomyxa, Stemonitis, Lycogala,* etc.

DIVISION EUMYCOPHYTA—38,000 species
True fungi: nongreen plants composed of branching, threadlike structures called hyphae and found wherever there is suitable food, moisture and temperature; include molds, mildews, yeasts, and mushrooms.

DIVISION BRYOPHYTA—22,320 species
Mosses, liverworts, and hornworts: inconspicuous, mostly land forms, few aquatic, many found on moist surfaces of tree trunks and rocks; include *Marchantia, Ricciocarpus, Anthoceros, Polytrichum,* etc.

DIVISION PSILOPHYTA—4 living species
Psilophytes: most primitive of the vascular plants; include mostly fossil species, two living genera, *Psilotum* and *Tmesipteris.*

DIVISION LEPIDOPHYTA—900 living species, 700 fossil species
Club mosses and quillworts: mostly tropical and subtropical species, some in temperate zones; include Ground Pine *(Lycopodium)* and *Selaginella.*

DIVISION CALAMOPHYTA—25 living species, 400 fossil species
Horsetails: plants with jointed stems found in marshy habitats throughout the world except in Australia; all living species included in the genus *Equisetum.*

DIVISION FILICOPHYTA—10,000 species
Ferns: a widely distributed plant group found from the tropics to the arctic; one of the oldest of plant groups with fossil species dating back 300 million years; include *Polypodium, Adiantum, Polystichum, Woodwardia,* etc.

DIVISION CYCADOPHYTA—100 species
Cycads: a small group of palm-like trees and shrubs found in the tropics and subtropics; includes four genera with *Zamia* found in Florida and Mexico.

DIVISION CONIFEROPHYTA—620 species
Conifers or evergreens: largest group of living gymnosperms, widely distributed familiar cone-bearing trees; include pines, junipers, cedars, cypresses, firs, etc.

DIVISION ANTHOPHYTA—250,000 species
Angiosperms or Flowering Plants: largest plant group, seed-forming plants widely distributed; include Monocotyledons (lilies, sedges, palms, grasses, orchids, etc.) and Dicotyledons (most of the familiar wildflowers, weeds, shrubs, and deciduous trees, etc.)

THE ANIMAL WORLD

The actual number of animals is not known. Zoologists think that there may be as many as 1,600,000 species. This includes all kinds from the microscopic Protozoa to the sponges, sea stars, and the larger birds, reptiles, and mammals. Entomologists believe that there may be as many as a million kinds of insects alone; many new ones are described each year by the specialists who are called taxonomists. And who shall say how many kinds of threadworms (nematodes) there are, or how many kinds of fishes? Sometimes the casual observer or the amateur naturalist discovers a new animal, but it is the specialist who knows best the animal group to which the newly discovered creature belongs, who gives the scientific name. A college student walking up a desert canyon recently found a new land snail among the rocks, but it was left to an eminent malacologist (a highly-trained student of mollusks) to tell him of the importance of his discovery, and to classify and name his snail.

Zoologists have divided the Animal Kingdom into three sub-kingdoms:

1. Eozoa*: very small animals composed of an individual mass of living matter (protoplasm). Each mass, usually a cell, carries on all the life processes.
2. Parazoa: the sponges, unique as animal organisms.
3. Histozoa (Metazoa): includes all remaining animals, from comb jellies to roundworms, sea stars, tunicates, fishes, reptiles, birds, and mammals.

*This group of one-celled animals is sometimes combined with the equivalent group of unicellular plants (one-celled algae and bacteria) to form the Protista, a term invented by the German biologist Ernst Haeckel to include all unicellular organisms.

Mammals

Reptiles

Birds

Amphibians

Bony Fishes

Arthropods

Sharks

Lampreys

Segmented Worms

Tunicates

Mollusks

Echinoderms

Flatworms

Roundworms

Moss Animals

Coelenterates

Protozoa

Sponges

The animal kingdom

These sub-kingdoms have been divided into major groups, or phyla, which are further divided into sub-phyla, classes, orders, families, genera, and species.

The most important phyla are described below, with additional minor phyla briefly mentioned.

PHYLUM PROTOZOA—30,000 species
Protozoans: mostly microscopic single-celled animals; require moist habitat; free-living, free-swimming, some sessile, some colonial, some parasitic; include flagellates, rhizopods, sporozoans, ciliates, suctorians.

PHYLUM PORIFERA—5,000 species
Sponges: multicellular animals; marine and freshwater forms, all sessile; include chalk sponges, glass sponges, horn sponges, bath sponges.

PHYLUM COELENTERATA—10,000 species
Coelenterates: single or colonial, all aquatic, chiefly marine forms; include jellyfishes, corals, sea anemones, hydroids.

PHYLUM PLATYHELMINTHES—10,000 species
Flatworms: some free-living forms inhabit moist earth or water and many animal parasites; include turbellarians, flukes, tapeworms.

PHYLUM NEMATODA—13,000 species
Roundworms: some free-living in fresh water, salt water, or soil; others parasitic in tissues or fluids of animals or plants; include hookworms, pinworms, trichina worms, root nematodes, ascaris, horsehair worms.

PHYLUM ECHINODERMATA—6,000 species
Echinoderms: all solitary marine forms; most free-living, some attached; include starfishes or sea stars, brittle stars, sea urchins, sea cucumbers, sand dollars, sea lilies, feather stars.

PHYLUM MOLLUSCA—70,000 species
Mollusks: mostly free-living marine forms, along seashores and in shallow waters; some freshwater species; include species of value to man such as abalone, clams, oysters, mussels, squid; major pests such as snails, slugs, shipworms; also chitons, limpets, nudibranchs, sea hares, toothshells, land snails.

PHYLUM ANNELIDA—6,500 species
Segmented worms: some in damp soil, others in fresh water, and one group in the ocean; some species free-living, others parasitic, some living in burrows or tubes; include earthworms, marine worms, leeches.

PHYLUM ARTHROPODA—1,000,000 species

Jointed-footed animals, or arthropods: the most ubiquitous phylum, occurring on land, soil, in fresh and salt water, and in air; free-living and parasitic forms; crawling, jumping, flying, and swimming forms; include crustaceans (crab, shrimp, etc.), insects, spiders and their relatives, centipedes, millipedes, etc., many species of great importance to man and other animals as food; others very important as destroyers of man's food, clothing, and shelter, and as carriers of disease to man.

PHYLUM CHORDATA—60,000 species

Lower chordates and vertebrates: free-living (except for tunicates) forms found in fresh and salt water, on land, underground in burrows, in trees, and in air; include marine tongue worms, sea squirts, lancelets, fishes, amphibians, reptiles, birds, mammals.

Additional minor phyla are given in the accompanying tabulation.

Phylum	Habitat	Species in group	Includes
Ctenophora	Marine	100	Comb jellies, sea walnuts
Nemertinea	Mostly marine	500	Ribbon worms
Entoprocta	Mostly marine	60	Entoprocts
Rotifera	Fresh-water	1,300	Rotifers or wheel animalcules
Gastrotricha	Marine and fresh-water	200	Gastrotrichs
Acanthocephala	Parasitic	300	Spiny-headed worms
Bryozoa	Mostly marine	2,500	Moss animals
Brachiopoda	Marine	225	Lamp shells
Phoronidea	Marine	15	Phoronids
Chaetognatha	Marine	30	Arrow worms
Sipunculoidea	Seashore burrows in sand or mud	250	Peanut worms
Priapuloidea	Mud or sand or shallow marine waters	3	Priapulids
Echiuroidea	Mud or sand or shallow marine waters	60	Echiurids

NAMING PLANTS AND ANIMALS

Naming objects is one of the oldest, most necessary, and most valuable pastimes in the world. To give a name is to identify and catalogue an object so that we may talk about it; it is a way of showing that we think it differs from other things which perhaps superficially it may resemble. Once we have carefully defined or particularized a plant or animal by giving it a name, we can successfully use that name to convey to others our ideas about it.

A really good name refers to a single thing, definitely identifying it. Ornithologists have adopted a single English name for each bird species, but unfortunately a similar set of names has not been adopted for plants. An example of the confusion that may be caused by a common name is "bull pine," which may refer to any of half a dozen different pines, depending on the locality. The name "ironwood" has been applied to at least twenty kinds of hardwood trees. Californians call their species of *Ceanothus* "wild lilacs," which is very misleading, since these shrubs are not lilacs at all, but belong to a different family of plants, the Buckthorn family (Rhamnaceae). And many different yellow wild flowers are indiscriminately called "buttercups." In southern California common names of plants found only east of the Mississippi River have been wrongly applied to wildflowers which only slightly resemble the eastern species and which often are not even closely related.

The same confusion arises from the vernacular names used for animals. In California, "gopher" refers to the Pocket Gopher, a burrowing rodent of orchards and gardens; in the Rocky Mountains, in the Midwest, and in western Canada the name "gopher" is applied to a small striped ground squirrel; while in Florida a land tortoise is a "gopher."

The use of scientific names would avoid this confusion, for there is just one correct scientific name for each animal or plant. A scientific name may be used in any part of the world and always refers to the same plant or animal.

In the California Natural History Guides, the common names for species begin with a capital letter, but general names that refer to groups of species or one or more genera are not capitalized. Thus the "w" in warbler is not capitalized, but the "L" and "W" in Lucy Warbler are. Scientific names are always italicized. Generally they are enclosed in parentheses; they always are when they follow a common name.

The scientific name of a plant or animal consists of two parts: the genus or generic name and the trivial or specific name. The generic name always begins with a capital letter and may be compared to one's family name (Jones, Smith, etc). The species or specific name is comparable to one's given name (Richard, James, etc.), and ordinarily begins with a lowercase letter. If the species name of a plant is commemorative, that is, perpetuates the name of a person (Watsoni, Parishii, etc.), it may begin with a capital

Rocky Shore:
Catalina Island

Coastal Strand: Goleta

Coastal Salt Marsh:
San Elijo Lagoon

Coastal Salt Marsh:
Del Mar

Santa Inez Canyon   Hidden Valley

Freshwater Marsh

Santa Inez River   Palm Canyon

Riparian Woodland

Santa Inez Canyon   Riverside County

Coastal Scrub

Chaparral:
San Marcos Pass

Southern Oak Woodland:
Santa Barbara County

Cismontane Urban:
La Jolla

Cismontane Rural:
San Diego County

Piñon—Juniper Woodland: Piñon Flat

Yellow Pine Forest: above Barton Flats   *Lodgepole Pine—White Fir Forest: Mt. San Gorgonio*

Mountain Meadow: Slushy Meadow, Mt. San Gorgonio

Alpine Fell:
Summit, Mt. San Gorgonio

Joshua Tree—High Desert
Woodland:
Teenach Joshua Tree Forest

Sagebrush Scrub:
Owens Valley

Sagebrush Scrub:
Owens Valley

Creosote Bush—Low Desert Scrub

Riverside County

Creosote Bush—Low Desert Scrub

Riverside County

Desert Sand Dunes:
Coachella Valley

Desert Sand Dunes:
Algodones

Desert Wash: Box Canyon

Shadscale Scrub:
Owens Valley

Alkali Sink:
Owens Lake

Salt-Water Lake:
Salton Sea

Desert Canal:
Imperial Valley

Colorado River Bottom:
Colorado River

Desert Urban:
Palm Springs

Desert Rural:
Coachella Valley

letter. One of our common birds, the Roadrunner, has the scientific name *Geococcyx californianus,* literally "California ground cuckoo." The generic name is derived from Greek stems; the specific name is "california" with a Latin ending. Every scientific name was coined by the person who described the animal or plant, and we usually place the person's family name or an abbreviation of it after the scientific name. Thus, *Geococcyx californianus* (Lesson), or *Geococcyx californianus* (Less.).

The complete classification of the Mourning Dove is as follows:
Kingdom: Animal
  Subkingdom: Metazoa
    Phylum: Chordata
      Subphylum: Gnathostomata
        Class: Aves
          Order: Columbiformes
           Family: Columbidae
             Genus: *Zenaidura*
              Species: *macroura*

The scientific name of this dove is *Zenaidura macroura* (Linn.).

The complete scientific classification for the California Poppy is as follows:
Kingdom: Plant
  Subkingdom: Embryophyta
    Division: Tracheophyta
      Subdivision: Pteropsida
        Class: Angiospermae
          Subclass: Dicotyledonae
           Order: Rhoeadales
             Family: Papaveraceae
              Genus: *Eschscholtzia*
              Species: *californica*

The scientific names of this wild poppy then is *Eschscholtzia californica* (Cham.).

Plants and animals can be identified in many ways. Perhaps the simplest is to go into the field with an expert and have him point out the living plant or animal in its natural habitat, tell you its scientific name, and teach you the characteristics that distinguish it from others. Much help can be obtained on field trips of the local Audubon Society or other nature groups. Some state, regional, and city parks offer nature talks and walks along special trails with signs to identify the natural features.

Some plants and animals can be collected and compared with identified museum specimens or with illustrations in guidebooks. The museum specimen or illustration most closely resembling the collected specimen is found by careful search. After arriving at a tentative identification, you may be able to name the specimen in hand by comparing its size, form, color, anatomy, and range with a museum specimen or book entry. This method can be used successfully for distinctive species and for those with few close relatives.

To identify some specimens, however, you must use artificial devices called identification keys. In these keys the characteristics (usually anatomical) are arranged in lettered or numbered pairs. By progressively choosing the characteristic that applies to the specimen in hand (or perched in the bush), you arrive at the correct name of the specimen. A numbered key for certain familiar objects is as follows:

1. Objects made of wood; with or without metal parts............ 2
   Objects made of glass 5
2. With legs 3
   Without legs 4
3. With four legs and a large rectangular
   flat top; without metal parts ....table
   With three legs and a small circular
   flat top; with metal parts ....Camera tripod
4. Large, with a series of parallel
   horizontal boards ....Bookshelf
   Small, enclosed on all six sides; with
   one side that can be opened ....Cigar box

5. Transparent ....Window
   Opaque, silvered on one side ....Mirror

To use the above key for identifying one of the pictured objects, choose one of the descriptions in the first couplet. Depending on your choice, you then proceed to couplet 2 or 5 and repeat the process. When you reach a description with a name opposite, you have "keyed" or identified the object.

A simple lettered key for identifying major insect groups might read, in part, as follows:

  A. With two wings (one pair) ....Flies
 AA. With four wings (two pair) ....B or BB
   B. Forewings hard and leathery; without veins ....Beetles
 BB. All four wings of equal consistency and veined......C or CC
   C. Wings covered with tiny scales; mouthparts modified into a long tube for sucking that is coiled beneath head ....Butterflies
                                               and Moths
CC. Wings without scales; clear and membranous...........Ants, bees, or wasps

Many natural history books contain identification keys of this kind. Some keys include drawings of the key characters. An extensive series of popular identification manuals using keys with drawings is the *Pictured Key Nature Series*, edited by H. E. Jacques, Dubuque, Iowa: Wm. C. Brown Co.

LIFE ZONES AND BIOTIC COMMUNITIES

As you climb the high mountains you will notice definite changes in the vegetational cover and temperature from the lower basal slopes to higher elevations. If the slopes are very steep, the changes may be abrupt and easily recognizable. Trees and shrubs of the lower areas, such as Western Sycamore, live oaks, and Chamise, are replaced at higher cooler elevations by deciduous oaks, Yellow Pines, Incense Cedar, and White Fir. At still greater heights (about 8,500 ft.) these trees thin out and give place to Lodgepole Pine forests and scattered Limber Pines. There is a definite zonation, a division into climatic belts of varying width, each with its peculiar temperature, humidity, trees, shrubs, and annual plants. Note that animal life also changes as you ascend the slopes. Birds and mammals at lower levels are very different from those which live on the summits.

Biologists putting all of this in order came up with what they called the life-zone concept.

In southern California biologists recognized three major life zones: the Sonoran, the Transition, and the Boreal, with its subdivisions. (See diagram, pp. 40-41).

The *Lower Sonoran Life Zone* is best represented on the Colorado and Mojave deserts. The ranges and intervening basins are areas of high summer temperature, high aridity, and little rainfall (2-5 in.) unevenly distributed. Typical plants are the Creosote Bush, Burrobush, Desert Willow, and Ironwood Tree. Elevations vary from below sea level to 3,000 feet.

The *Upper Sonoran* life zone varies from near sea level to 5,000 feet, and is best represented in the cismontane valleys and low mountain slopes covered with chaparral. The rainfall, highest in winter, varies from 5 to 15 inches. Typical plants are Scrub Oak, California Juniper, Chamise, and Piñon Pine (on desert slopes only). Common animals are Coyote, Gray Fox, Brush Rabbit, and Spotted Skunk.

The *Transition* life zone, at elevations of 5,000 to 7,500 feet, is the zone of the Ponderosa or Yellow Pine, California Black Oak, and Sugar Pine. Representative mammals are the Western Gray Squirrel, Merriam's Chipmunk, Mountain Chickadee, and Acorn Woodpecker.

The *Boreal* life zone is divided into (1) the *Canadian-Hudsonian* life zone with Lodgepole Pine, Limber Pine, and Chinquapin as representative trees and shrubs, and the Lodgepole Chipmunk and Clark's Nutcracker as typical animals, at altitudes from 8,000 to 10,000 feet; and (2) the *Arctic Alpine* life zone, found only on the summits of San Gorgonio and San Jacinto peaks. The latter summit represents the southern limit of Arctic-Alpine conditions in the United States. (See pp. 85-86). A few stunted Limber Pines and some northern perennials here withstand the strong winds and unfavorable conditions.

To discover the life zones, climb Mount San Jacinto* from Palm Desert, in the Lower Sonoran life zone, to the summit in the Boreal zone—by auto over the Palms-to-Pines Highway (74) to Idyllwild in the Transition zone, and by foot to the peak. A trip to the summit of Mount San Gorgonio also reveals the full sequence of zones. The warming influence of the desert consistently forces upward and narrows the life zones on the northern and eastern slopes of both mountains.

Life zones are based primarily on differences in temperature, but we now realize that to explain adequately the distribution of animals and plants we must consider many other factors, in addition to temp-

___

* The 8516 foot level may also be reached from Chino Canyon by the Palm Springs Aerial Tramway.

erature. The distribution of animals is affected by available food and shelter, competition for food, light, cloudiness, density of the atmosphere, and other factors.

Biologists now recognize another classification based on all these factors combined. They speak of naturally-occurring groups of different organisms (plant and animals), inhabiting a common environment and interacting with each other, especially through food relationships, as a "biotic community." Biotic communities may be large or small; they are not always clearly defined, since they frequently merge into each other. Nevertheless they are usually recognizable.

The largest and most important biotic communities of Southern California are described in the next section.

For color illustrations typical of these biotic communities see the plate section.

BIOTIC COMMUNITIES OF
SOUTHERN CALIFORNIA

1. ROCKY SHORE:
Location and examples:
Surf-beaten rocky beaches, shores, and sea cliffs along Pacific coast from Morro Bay to San Diego. A narrow strip between low tide and shoreline where sands and rocks are often wet or damp. Examples: coasts near San Onofre, Laguna Beach, La Jolla, Malibu, Palos Verdes Hills, Dana Point, and Santa Barbara where reefs and rock formations extend from shore.
Characteristic plants:
Surf grasses *(Phyllospadix torreyi, P. scouleri)*, Sea Lettuce *(Ulva lactuca)*, and numerous other marine plants.
Characteristic animals:
Birds: Black Turnstone *(Arenaria melanocephala)*, Surfbird *(Aphriza virgata)*, Wandering Tattler *(Heteroscelus incanum)*, Spotted Sandpiper *(Acitis macularia)*, Western Gull *(Larus occidentalis)*, Heerman's Gull *(Laurus heermani)*.
Invertebrates: great variety including Acorn Barnacle *(Balanus tintinnabulum, B. glandula)*, a beach flea or hopper *(Orchestoidea columbiana)*, an isopod *(Lygida occidentalis)*, Lined Shore Crab *(Pachygrapsus crassipes)*.

2. COASTAL STRAND:
Location and examples:
Sandy beaches and coastal dunes. A narrow community of limited areas with high humidity, frequent fogs, and low summer rainfall. Examples: Coronado Beach, San Clemente Beach, Santa Barbara Beach, Goleta dunes.
Characteristic plants:
Low or prostrate, often succulent woody perennials. Shore Sandbur *(Franseria chamissonis bipinnatisecta)*, White-leafed Saltbush *(Atriplex leucophylla)*, iceplants *(Mesembryanthemum nodiflorum, M. crystallinum, M. chilense)*, a lupine *(Lupinus chamissonis)*, Haplopappus ericoides.
Characteristic animals:

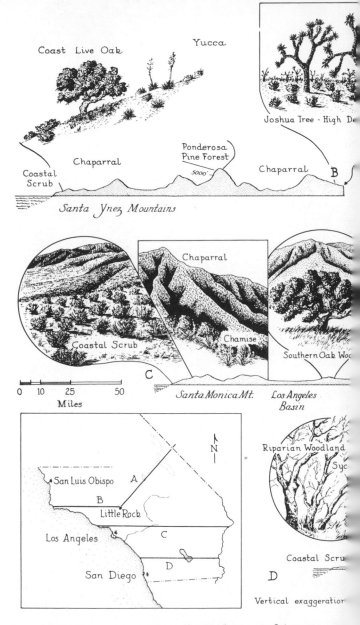

Coast Live Oak

Yucca

Joshua Tree - High De

Ponderosa
Pine Forest

Chaparral

5000'

Chaparral

B

Coastal
Scrub

Santa Ynez Mountains

Chaparral

Coastal Scrub

Chamise

Southern Oak Woo

C

Santa Monica Mt.

*Los Angeles
Basin*

0 10   25   50
        Miles

San Luis Obispo

A

B

Little Rock

Los Angeles

C

D

San Diego

N

Riparian Woodland

Syc

Coastal Scru

D

Vertical exaggeration

Biotic communities of southern California

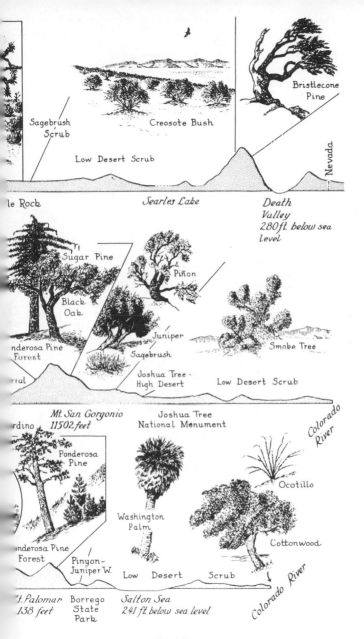

Sagebrush Scrub

Creosote Bush

Bristlecone Pine

Low Desert Scrub

Nevada

le Rock

Searles Lake

Death Valley 280 ft. below sea level

Sugar Pine

Black Oak

Piñon

Juniper

nderosa Pine Forest

Sagebrush

Smoke Tree

rral

Joshua Tree - High Desert

Low Desert Scrub

Mt. San Gorgonio 11502 feet

Joshua Tree National Monument

Colorado River

dino

Ponderosa Pine

Ocotillo

Washington Palm

Cottonwood

nderosa Pine Forest

Pinyon-Juniper W.

Low Desert Scrub

Colorado River

t. Palomar 138 feet

Borrego State Park

Salton Sea 241 ft below sea level

Birds: Western Gull *(Larus occidentalis)*, California Gull *(Larus californicus)*, Sanderling *(Crocethia alba)*, Snowy Plover *(Charadrius alexandrinus)*.

Invertebrates: a sand crab *(Emerita analoga)*, a rove beetle *(Thinopinus pictus)*, tiger beetles *(Cicindela* spp.), beach amphipods or "fleas" *(Orchestia traskiana, Orchestoidea californica, O. columbiana)*, a butterfly, Square-spotted Blue *(Philotes battoides)*.

3. COASTAL SALT MARSH:

Location and examples:

A narrow strip of tidal lagoons and salt marshes, including intertidal mudflats, with low herbs or shrubs, often succulent, and a few perennial grasses. Examples: Sunset Beach, Bolsa Bay, Solana Beach, Mugu Lagoon, mouths of Santa Clara, Santa Margarita, and San Diegito rivers, Morro Bay.

Characteristic plants:

Sea Blite or Inkweed *(Sueda californica)*, pickleweeds *(Salicornia* spp.), Sea Heath *(Frankenia grandiflora)*, Salt Grass *(Distichlis spicata)*, Cord Grass *(Spartina foliosa)*.

Characteristic animals:

Mammals: California Vole *(Microtus californicus)*, Norway Rat *(Rattus norvegicus)*, House Mouse *(Mus musculus)*.

Birds: Clapper Rail *(Rallus longirostris)*, Common Egret *(Casmerodius albus)*, Snowy Egret *(Leucophoyx thula)*, Marsh Hawk *(Circus cyaneus)*, Savannah Sparrow *(Passerculus sandwichensis)*, American Avocet *(Recurvirostra americana)*, Willet *(Catoptrophorus semipalmatus)*, Western Sandpiper *(Ereunetes mauri)*, and many other shorebirds.

Invertebrates: Saltmarsh Fly *(Ephydra riparia)*, saltmarsh mosquitoes *(Aedes* spp.), butterflies, Pigmy Blue *(Brephidium exilis)*, Sandhill Skipper *(Polites sabuleti)*, Wandering Skipper *(Panoquina panoquinoides errans)*.

4. FRESHWATER MARSH:

Location and examples:

This community is scattered throughout southern California wherever shallow standing water remains any length of time. Small areas along coast in back of brackish areas, around springs, ponds, and lakes, and along sluggish streams. Examples: Santa Inez River, Lake Hodges, Prado Basin, Hidden Valley (near Corona).

Characteristic plants:

Common Tule *(Scirpus acutus)*, California Bulrush *(Scirpus californicus)*, Cat-tails *(Typha latifolia, T. angustifolia)*, spike rushes *(Eleocharis* spp.) pondweeds *(Potamogeton* spp.), sedges *(Carex* spp.).

Characteristic animals:

Birds: Common Gallinule *(Gallinula chloropus)*, American Coot *(Fulica americana)*, Long-billed Marsh Wren *(Telmatodytes palustris)*, Redwinged Blackbird *(Agelaius phoeniceus)*, Yellowthroat *(Geothlypis trichas)*.

Reptiles and amphibians: Garter Snake *(Thamnophis spp.)*. Western Pond Turtle *(Clemmys marmorata)*, Pacific Treefrog *(Hyla regilla)*.

Invertebrates: great variety of aquatic or semi-aquatic insects including predaceous diving beetles *(Dytiscus spp.)*, Giant Water Bug *(Lethocerus americanus)*, toadbug *(Gelastocoris variegatus)*.

5. RIPARIAN (STREAMSIDE) WOODLAND:

Location and examples:

Streams leading from mountains to cismontane plains and many smaller streams in mountain areas. Examples: Santa Inez River, Santa Clara River, Santa Ana River, San Luis Rey River, Manzana Creek, Sespe Creek, Lytle Creek, Palm Canyon.

Characteristic plants:

Big Cone Spruce *(Pseudotsuga macrocarpa)*, White Alder *(Alnus rhombifolia)*, Bigleaf Maple *(Acer macrophyllum)*, Western Sycamore *(Platanus racemosa)*, Western Red-bud *(Cercis occidentalis)*, Black Cottonwood *(Populus trichocarpa)*, Fremont Cottonwood *(Populus fremontii)*, willows *(Salix spp.)*.

Characteristic animals:

Mammals: Raccoon *(Procyon lotor)*, Striped Skunk *(Mephitis mephitis)*, Dusky-footed Woodrat *(Neotoma fuscipes)*.

Birds: Belted Kingfisher *(Megaceryle alcyon)*, Dipper or Water Ouzel *(Cinclus mexicanus)*, Yellow-breasted Chat *(Icteria virens)*, Yellow Warbler *(Dendroica petechia)*, Western Flycatcher *(Empidonax difficilis)*, Song Sparrow *(Melospiza melodia)*, House Wren *(Troglodytes aedon)*.

Reptiles and amphibians: Common Garter Snake *(Thamnophis sirtalis)*, Western Pond Turtle *(Clemmys marmorata)*, Southwestern Toad *(Bufo microscaphus)*, Ensatina *(Ensatina eschscholtzi)*.

Invertebrates: Western Tiger Swallowtail *(Papilio rutulus)*, Lorquin's Admiral *(Basilarchia lorquini)*, Satyr Anglewing *(Polygonia satyrus)*, Sylvan Hairstreak *(Strymon sylvinus)*.

6. COASTAL SCRUB:

Location and examples:

Well-drained clay or gravelly, sometimes rocky or rock-strewn, slopes of cismontane areas between sea and rather abruptly rising mountainous, chaparral-covered slopes, from San Luis Obispo County southward through San Diego County,

Examples: south- and west-facing slopes of steep hills back of San Luis Obispo, Santa Barbara, Fillmore, San Clemente, Claremont, and Riverside.

Characteristic plants:

California Wormwood or Sagebrush *(Artemisia californica)*, White Sage *(Salvia apiana)*, Black Sage *(Salvia mellifera)*, Encelia *(Encelia farinosa)*, Yerba Santa *(Eriodictyon californica)*, Eriophyllum *(Eriophyllum confertiflorum)*, California Buckwheat *(Eriogonum fasciculatum)*, Lemonade-berry *(Rhus integrifolia)*, Prickly pears *(Opuntia* spp.), Our Lord's Candle *(Yucca whipplei)*.

Mammals: California Ground Squirrel *(Citellus beecheyi)*, Nimble Kangaroo Rat *(Dipodomys agilis)*, Desert Wood Rat *(Neotoma lepida)*, California Mouse *(Peromyscus californicus)*, Short-eared Pocket Mouse *(Perognathus fallax)* (Los Angeles County southward).

Birds: Costa's Hummingbird *(Calypte costae)*, Cactus Wren *(Campylorhynchus brunneicapillum)*, Lazuli Bunting *(Passerina amoena)*, Wrentit *(Chamaea fasciata)*, Brown Towhee *(Pipilo fuscus)*, Sage Sparrow *(Amphispiza belli)*, Rufous-crowned Sparrow *(Aimophila ruficeps)*.

Reptiles: Western Fence Lizard *(Sceloporus occidentalis)*, Striped Racer *(Masticophis lateralis)*, Western Rattlesnake *(Crotalus viridis)*.

Invertebrates: Ringlet *(Coenonympha tullia)*, Common Checkspot *(Euphydryas chalcedona)*, Leanira Checkerspot *(Melitaea leanira)*, Bramble Hairstreak *(Callophrys dumetorum)*, Mormon Metalmark *(Apodemia mormo)*.

7. CHAPARRAL:

Location and examples:

Best developed of southern California plant communities. Dense cover of shrubs up to 15 feet high, of plains, mesas, and foothills; particularly well developed on coastal side of mountains from San Luis Obispo County southward into Lower California at 1,000 to 4,000 feet, 3,000 to 5,500 feet on desert side of mountains; great diversity of evergreen shrubs often with thick leathery leaves; many shrubs have fire-resistant seeds of long viability and sprout quickly from roots after fires.

Characteristic plants:

Chamise *(Adenostoma fasciculatum)*, Scrub Oak *(Quercus dumosa)*, Foothill Ash *(Fraxinus dipetala)*, Hard Tack *(Cercocarpus betuloides)*, wild lilacs *(Ceanothus cordulatus, C. greggii, C. leucodermis, C. megacarpus, C. crassifolius*, etc.), Holly-leaf Cherry *(Prunus ilicifolia)*, Bear Brush *(Garrya fremontii)*, Quinine Bush *(Garrya flavescens)*, manzanitas *(Arctostaphylos pun-*

[44]

gens, A. pringlei, A. glauca, A. glandulosa, etc), Toyon (*Heteromeles arbutifolia*), Sugarbush (*Rhus ovata*).

Characteristic animals:

Mammals: Mule Deer (*Odocoileus hemionus*), Coyote (*Canis latrans*), Gray Fox (*Urocyon cinereoargenteus*), Bobcat (*Lynx rufus*), Brush Rabbit (*Sylvilagus bachmanni*), Dusky-footed Woodrat (*Neotoma fuscipes*), Nimble Kangaroo Rat (*Dipodomys agilis*), California Pocket Mouse (*Perognathus californicus*), California Mouse (*Peromyscus californicus*).

Birds: Mountain Quail (*Oreortyx pictus*), Scrub Jay (*Aphelocoma coerulescens*), Wrentit (*Chamaea fasciata*), Poor-will (*Phalaenoptilus nuttallii*), Bewick's Wren (*Thryomanes bewickii*), California Thrasher (*Toxostoma redivivum*), Rufous-sided Towhee (*Pipilo erythrophthalmus*), Orange-crowned Warbler (*Vermivora celata*).

Reptiles: Western Fence Lizard (*Sceloporus occidentalis*), Southern Alligator Lizard (*Gerrhonotus multicarinatus*), Coast Horned Lizard (*Phrynosoma coronatum*), Striped Racer (*Masticophis lateralis*), Western Rattlesnake (*Crotalus viridis*).

Invertebrates: Ceanothus Silk Moth (*Platysamia euryalus*), another silk moth (*Saturnia walterorum*), Gray Hairstreak (*Strymon adenostomatis*), Hedge-Row Hairstreak (*Strymon saepium*), Arota Copper (*Lycaena arota*), Callippe Fritillary (*Speyeria callippe*), a flat-headed borer or buprestid (*Acmaeodera mariposa*), California Timema (*Timema californica*).

8. SOUTHERN OAK (FOOTHILL) WOODLAND:

Location and examples:

Dense to open forest, trees 15–75 feet high, with scattered shrubs and grassland in foothills. Examples: oak parklands back of Santa Barbara, Ojai, Pasadena, Warner's Ranch in eastern Riverside County, Ramona and vicinity in San Diego county, cismontane mountain borders and north foothill slopes in San Bernardino County.

Characteristic plants:

Big-cone Spruce (*Pseudotsuga macrocarpa*), Digger Pine (*Pinus sabiniana*) (from Los Angeles County north), Coulter Pine (*Pinus coulteri*), California Juniper (*Juniperus californica*), California Black Walnut (*Juglans californica*), Coast Live Oak (*Quercus agrifolia*), Englemann Oak (*Quercus englemannii*), Interior Live Oak (*Quercus wislizenii*), gooseberry (*Ribes quercetorum*), Sugar Bush (*Rhus ovata*), Lemonade-berry (*Rhus integrifolia*), Squaw Bush (*Rhus trilobata*), Bigberry Manzanita (*Arctostaphylos glauca*), Wild Oats (*Avena fatua*), Wild Mountain Sunflower (*Helianthus gracilentus*).

Characteristic animals:

Mammals: Mule Deer *(Odocoileus hemionus)*, Raccoon *(Procyon lotor)*, Gray Fox *(Urocyon cinereoargenteus)*, Western Gray Squirrel *(Sciurus griseus)*, Dusky-footed Woodrat *(Neotoma fuscipes)*, California Mouse *(Peromyscus californicus)*, Brush Mouse *(P. boylii)*.

Birds: California Quail *(Lophortyx californicus)*, Acorn Woodpecker *(Melanerpes formicivorus)*, Scrub Jay *(Aphelocoma coerulescens)*, Plain Titmouse *(Parus inornatus)*, Common Bushtit *(Psaltriparus minimus)*, Black-headed Grosbeak *(Pheucticus melanocephalus)*.

Reptiles: Western Fence Lizard *(Sceloporus occidentalis)*, Skinks *(Eumeces skiltonianus, E. gilberti)*, California Mountain Kingsnake *(Lampropeltis zonata)*, Red Rattlesnake *(Crotalus ruber)* (San Gorgonia Pass southward).

Invertebrates: Sister *(Limenitis bredowi)*, Callippe Silverspot *(Speyeria callippe)*, Ringlet *(Coenonympha tullia)*, Sylvan Satyr *(Cercyonis silvestris)*, California Hairstreak *(Strymon californica)*, California Oak Moth *(Phryganidia californica)*, Brown Ctenucha *(Ctenucha brunnea)*, Snowy Tree Cricket *(Oecanthus niveus)*, California Timema *(Timema californica)*.

9. CISMONTANE (COASTAL) URBAN:

Location and examples:
Cities and towns of coastal areas with residential subdivisions, parks, cemeteries, and vacant lots.

Characteristic plants:
A great variety of introduced trees, shrubs, and garden flowers, many from Mediterranean region, South Africa, South America, Australia, and East Asia. Also native trees from northern California and eastern United States.

Characteristic animals:
Mammals: Opossum *(Didelphis marsupialis virginiana)*, Southern Pocket Gopher *(Thomomys bottae)*, Norway Rat *(Rattus norvegicus)*, Black Rat *(Rattus rattus)*, House Mouse *(Mus musculus)*.

Birds: Barn Owl *(Tyto alba)*, Mourning Dove *(Zenaidura macroura)*, Spotted Dove *(Streptopelia chinensis)*, Rock Dove or Domestic Pigeon *(Columba livia)*, Mockingbird *(Mimus polyglottos)*, Brewer's Blackbird *(Euphagus cyanocephalus)*, House Sparrow *(Passer domesticus)*, House Finch *(Carpodacus mexicanus)*, Brown Towhee *(Pipilo fuscus)*.

Invertebrates: Garden Snail *(Helix aspersa)*, sowbug *(Porcellio laevis)*, West Coast Lady *(Vanessa caryae)*, Buckeye *(Precis orithya)*, Gulf Fritillary *(Agraulis vanillae)*, House Fly *(Musca domestica)*.

10. CISMONTANE (COASTAL) RURAL:

Location and examples:

Cultivated croplands, pastures, fruit and nut orchards, alfalfa fields, garden produce fields, vineyards; mostly on valley floors where irrigation is available. Extensive areas from San Luis Obispo County to San Diego County.

Characteristic plants:

Celery *(Apium graveolens)*, Tomato *(Lycopersicon esculentum)*, Cauliflower *(Brassica oleracea* var. *botrytis)*, Head Lettuce *(Lactuca sativa* var. *capitata)*, Almond *(Prunus amygdalus)*, Peach *(Prunus persica)*, Orange *(Citrus sinensis)*, Lemon *(Citrus limon)*, Potato *(Solanum tuberosum)*, Wine Grape *(Vitis vinifera)*.

Characteristic animals:

Mammals: Opossum *(Didelphis marsupialis virginiana)*, Striped Skunk *(Mephitis mephitis)*, Coyote *(Canis latrans)*, Black-tailed Jackrabbit *(Lepus californicus)*, California Ground Squirrel *(Citellus beecheyi)*, Southern Pocket Gopher *(Thomomys bottae)*, Deer Mouse *(Peromyscus maniculatus)*, House Mouse *(Mus musculus)*.

Birds: Sparrow Hawk *(Falco sparverius)*, Western Kingbird *(Tyrannus verticalis)*, Mourning Dove *(Zenaidura macroura)*, Horned Lark *(Eremophila alpestris)*, Mockingbird *(Mimus polyglottos)*, Loggerhead Shrike *(Lanius ludovicianus)*, Western Meadowlark *(Sturnella neglecta)*, Brown Towhee *(Pipilo fuscus)*.

Reptiles: Gopher Snake *(Pituophis melanoleucus)*.

Invertebrates: Painted Lady *(Vanessa cardui)*, Alfalfa Butterfly *(Colias eurytheme)*, Monarch *(Danaus plexippus)*, Jerusalem Cricket *(Stenopelmatus longispinis)*.

11. PINON-JUNIPER WOODLAND:

Location and examples:

Below Yellow Pine forests on desert side of Transverse Ranges at 3,500 to 6,000 feet. Found on crests of New York, Old Woman, Grapevine, Granite, Providence, Kingston, Clark, and Ivanpah Mountains of Mojave Desert; also desert slopes of San Jacinto, Santa Rosa, and Laguna Mountains. Trees 10—30 feet tall in open stands, often mixed with shrubs. A forest supporting few fires.

Characteristic plants:

One-leaf Piñon Pine *(Pinus monophylla)*, California Juniper *(Juniperus californica)*, Utah Juniper *(J. oteosperma)*, Scrub Oak *(Quercus dumosa)*, Black Bush *(Purshia glandulosa)*, Box Thorn *(Lycium cooperi)*, Mojave Yucca *(Yucca schidigera)*, Silver Cholla *(Opuntia echinocarpa)*, Desert Bunch Grass *(Stipa speciosa)*.

Characteristic animals:
Mammals: Coyote *(Canis latrans)*, Black-tailed Jackrabbit *(Lepus californicus)*, California Ground Squirrel *(Citellus beecheyi)*, Southern Pocket Gopher *(Thomomys bottae)*, Piñon Mouse *(Peromyscus truei)*.

Birds: Ladder-backed Woodpecker *(Dendrocopos scalaris)*, Piñon Jay *(Gymnorhinus cyanocephala)*, Rock Wren *(Salpinctes obsoletus)*, Poor-will *(Phalaenoptilus nuttallii)*, Black-throated Gray Warbler *(Dendroica nigrescens)*, Gray Vireo *(Vireo vicinior)*.

Reptiles: Speckled Rattlesnake *(Crotalus mitchelli)*.

Invertebrates: Juniper Hairstreak *(Mitoura siva)* (north of Riverside), Skinner's Hairstreak *(Mitoura loki)* (south of Riverside), Yucca Weevil *(Scyphophorus yuccae)*.

12. YELLOW PINE (PONDEROSA) FOREST:
Location and examples:
Mountain areas at 4,500 to 7,500 feet except for certain Death Valley mountains such as Panamints and Clark and Kingston Mountains; the higher mountains of Santa Barbara, Ventura, Los Angeles, San Bernardino, Riverside, and San Diego counties. Trees 50–120 feet tall in extensive almost continuous open forests. Some shrubs in spaces between trees, especially in lower parts of forests or where fire has destroyed the trees.

Characteristic plants:
Western Yellow Pine *(Pinus ponderosa)*, Jeffrey Pine *(Pinus jeffreyi)*, Sugar Pine *(Pinus lambertiana)*, Incense Cedar *(Libocedrus decurrens)*, White Fir *(Abies concolor)*, California Black Oak *(Quercus kelloggii)*, Mountain Mahogany *(Cercocarpus ledifolius)*, Manzanitas *(Arctostaphylos spp.)*.

Characteristic animals:
Mammals: Mule Deer *(Odocoileus hemionus)*, Western Gray Squirrel *(Sciurus griseus)*, Merriam's Chipmunk *(Eutamias merriami)*, Deer Mouse *(Peromyscus maniculatus)*.

Birds: Hairy Woodpecker *(Dendrocopos villosus)*, White-headed Woodpecker *(D. albolarvatus)*, Western Woodpewee *(Contopus sordidulus)*, Steller's Jay *(Cyanocitta stelleri)*, Band-tailed Pigeon *(Columba fasciata)*, Mountain Chickadee *(Parus gambeli)*, Pigmy Nuthatch *(Sitta pygmaea)*, Audubon's Warbler *(Dendroica auduboni)*.

Reptiles: Western Fence Lizard *(Sceloporus occidentalis)*, Western Rattlesnake *(Crotalus viridis)*, California Mountain Kingsnake *(Lampropeltis zonata)*.

Invertebrates: Semiramis Fritillary *(Speyeria coronis semiramis)*, a day-flying moth *(Gnophaela latipennis)*.

13. LODGEPOLE PINE—WHITE FIR FOREST:
  Location and examples:
  From 6,500 feet, but generally above 8,000 feet. Trees usually
  60—75 feet tall, sometimes in small dense stands. Near summits
  of San Gabriel, San Bernardino, and San Jacinto mountains.
  Clark Mountain in eastern San Bernardino County (firs only).
  Characteristic plants:
  White Fir *(Abies concolor)*, Murray or Lodgepole Pine *(Pinus
  murryana)*, Jeffrey Pine *(Pinus jeffreyi)*, Limber Pine *(Pinus
  flexilis)*, Bush Chinquapin *(Castanopsis sempervirens)*, Snow-
  brush *(Ceanothus cordulatus)*, Green Manzanita *(Arctostaphylos
  patula)*.
  Characteristic animals:
  Mammals: Lodgepole Chipmunk *(Eutamias speciosus)*,
  Golden-mantled Ground Squirrel *(Citellus lateralis)*, Deer
  Mouse *(Peromyscus maniculatus)*, Long-tailed Meadow Mouse
  (Microtus longicaudus).
  Birds: Williamson's Sapsucker *(Sphyrapicus thyroideus)*,
  Clark's Nutcracker *(Nucifraga columbiana)*, Dusky Flycatcher
  (Empidonax oberholseri), Ruby-crowned Kinglet *(Regulus calen-
  dula)*, Olive-sided Flycatcher *(Nuttallornis borealis)*, Cassin's
  Finch *(Carpodacus cassinii)*.
  Reptiles: Sagebrush Lizard *(Sceloporus graciosus)*.

14. MOUNTAIN MEADOW:
  Grassy swales or flats often dissected by small streams.
  Mostly at elevation of Yellow Pine forest or Lodgepole Pine—
  White Fir zone, above 4,500 feet. Usually bordered by pines,
  firs, etc. Examples: Buff Lake, South Fork Meadows, Tahquitz
  Valley, Saunders Meadows, Big Meadows, Holcomb Valley
  Meadow, Slushy Meadow.
  Characteristic plants:
  Arroyo Willow *(Salix lasiolepis)*, Yellow Willow *(Salix lasi-
  andra)*, False Hellebore *(Veratrum californicum)*, Mimulus
  (Mimulus nasutus), Wild Iris *(Iris missouriensis)*, wire grasses
  (Junucus spp.).
  Characteristic animals:
  Mammals: Southern Pocket Gopher *(Thomomys bottae)*, Deer
  Mouse *(Peromyscus maniculatus)*, California Meadow Mouse
  (Microtus californicus), Long-tailed Meadow Mouse *(M. longi-
  caudus)*, Ornate Shrew *(Sorex ornatus)*.
  Birds: Western Bluebird *(Sialia mexicana)*, Mountain Blue-
  bird *(Sialia eurrucoides)*, Wilson's Warbler *(Wilsonia pusilla)*.
  Amphibians: Pacific Treefrog *(Hyla regilla)*.
  Invertebrates: Sheep Moth *(Pseudohazis eglanterina)*, Green-
  ish Blue *(Plobojus saepiolus)*.

15. ALPINE FELL:
   Location and examples:
   Mostly above line of tree growth. Much of precipitation in form of snow. Frequent high winds. Some low and krummholz trees. Highest parts of Mount San Gorgonio, San Bernardino Peak, and Mount San Jacinto.
   Characteristic plants:
   Many compact perennial herbs such as Mountain Sorrel *(Oxyria digyna)*, Mountain Fleabane *(Erigeron compositus)*, Alpine Buttercup *(Ranunculus oxynotus)*, five-finger *(Potentilla wheeleri)*, Draba *(Draba corrugata)*. Also Limber Pine *(Pinus flexilis)*.
   Characteristic animals:
   Birds: Mountain Bluebird *(Sialia eurrucoides)*, Clark's Nutcracker *(Nucifraga columbiana)*, White-throated Swift *(Aeronautes saxatalis)*, Rock Wren *(Salpinctes obsoletus)*.

16. JOSHUA TREE—HIGH DESERT WOODLAND:
   Location and examples:
   Desert slopes of San Gabriel and San Bernardino mountains, Tehachapi Mountains, high mesas and valleys of eastern San Bernardino County (Cima Dome, Ivanpah Valley, Lanfair Valley, Mescal Range), and Joshua Tree National Monument.
   Characteristic plants:
   Joshua Tree *(Yucca brevifolia)*, Mojave Yucca *(Yucca schidigera)*, California Juniper *(Juniperus californica)*, Utah Juniper *(J. osteosperma)*, Paperbag Bush *(Salazaria mexicana)*, Spiny Tetradymia *(Tetradymia spinosa)*, Desert Bunch Grass *(Stipa speciosa)*, Galleta *(Hilaria rigida)*.
   Characteristic animals:
   Mammals: Merriam's Kangaroo Rat *(Dipodomys merriami)*, Desert Wood Rat *(Neotoma lepida)*, White-tailed Antelope Ground Squirrel *(Citellus leucurus)*.
   Birds: Piñon Jay *(Gymnorhinus cyanocephala)* Loggerhead Shrike *(Lanius ludovicianus)*, Scott's Oriole *(Icte̓ us parisorum)*.
   Reptiles: Chuckwalla *(Sauromalus obesus)*, Desert Night Lizard *(Xantusia vigilis)*, Desert Tortoise *(Gopherus agassizi)*,
   Invertebrates: Felder's Orange-tip *(Anthocharis cethura)*, Mormon Metalmark *(Apodemia morma)*, Mojave Blue *(Philotes mojave)*, Yucca Moths *(Pronuba spp.)*, Yucca Weevil *(Scyphophorus yuccae)*.

17. SAGEBRUSH SCRUB:
   Location and examples:
   Coarse gravel slopes and mesas between Piñon—Juniper

Woodland and Creosote Bush—Low Desert Scrub. Rainfall 6 to 8 inches, some snow in winter. North bases of San Gabriel and San Bernardino mountains and high desert (4,000—5,500 feet) or eastern San Bernardino and Inyo counties.

Characteristic plants:

Great Basin Sage *(Artemisia tridentata)*, Blackbush *(Coleogyne ramosissimma)*, Goldenbush or Rabbitbrush *(Chrysothamnus nauseosus)*, Four-wing Saltbush *(Atriplex canescens)*, Purple Sage *(Salvia dorii)*, Mojave Yucca *(Yucca schidigera)*, Spiny Tetradymia *(Tetradymia spinosa)*.

Characteristic animals:

Mammals: Black-tailed Jack Rabbit *(Lepus californicus)*, Desert Cottontail *(Sylvilagus auduboni)*, Deer Mouse *(Peromyscus maniculatus)*.

Birds: Green-tailed Towhee *(Chlorura chlorura)*, Sage Sparrow *(Amphispiza belli)*, Brewer's Sparrow *(Spizella breweri)*.

Reptiles: Side-blotched Lizard *(Uta stansburiana)*, Desert Horned Lizard *(Phrynosoma platyrhinos)*.

Invertebrates: darkling ground beetles *(Eleodes* spp.), Becker's White *(Pieris beckerii)*, Felder's Orange-tip *(Anthocharis cethura)*, Neumoegen's Checker-spot *(Melitaea neumoegeni)*, Cerambycid beetles *(Crossidius* spp.).

18. SHADSCALE SCRUB:

Location and examples:

Mesas and flat areas at 3,000 to 6,000 feet, average rainfall 3 to 7 inches, soil somewhat alkaline. Plants, mainly shrubs 1—4 feet tall, shallow-rooted and of a gray-green color, growing close together and occurring over wide areas. Northern Mojave Desert and Owens Valley.

Characteristic plants:

Shadscale *(Atriplex confertifolia)*, Hop-sage *(Grayia spinosa)*, Mulefat *(Eurotia lanata)*, Matchweed *(Gutierrezia sarothrae)*.

Characteristic animals:

Mammals: White-tailed Antelope Ground Squirrel *(Citellus leucurus)*, Black-tailed Jack Rabbit *(Lepus californicus)*, Merriams' Kangaroo Rat *(Dipodomys merriami)*, Chisel-toothed Kangaroo Rat *(Dipodomys microps)*, Desert Wood Rat *(Neotoma lepida)*.

Birds: Black-throated Sparrow *(Amphispiza bilineata)*.

Reptiles: Zebra-tailed Lizard *(Callisaurus draconoides)*, Gopher Snake *(Pituophis melanoleucus)*, Mojave Rattlesnake *(Crotalus scutulatus)* (not known from Owens Valley).

Invertebrates: San Emigdio Blue *(Plebejus emigdionis)*.

19. CREOSOTE BUSH—LOW DESERT SCRUB:

Location and examples:
Lower slopes, alluvial fans and valleys of low desert country from about 3,000 feet to below sea level. Plants, mainly shrubs 3 to 9 feet tall, growing far apart but over wide areas. Covers most of southern Mojave Desert and Colorado Desert.

Characteristic plants:
Creosote Bush *(Larrea divaricata)*, Burrobush *(Franseria dumosa)*, Indigo Bush *(Dalea shottii)*, Dye Bush *(Dalea emoryi)*, Brittlebush *(Encelia farinosa),* Desert Lily *(Hesperocallis undulata)*, Ocotillo *(Fouquieria splendens)*, Bigelow's Cholla *(Opuntia bigelovii)*, Silver Cholla *(O. echinocarpa)*, Englemann's Cereus *(Cereus englemannii)*.

Characteristic animals:
Mammals: White-tailed Antelope Ground Squirrel *(Citellus leucurus)*, Round-tailed Ground Squirrel *(Citellus tereticaudus)*, Black-tailed Jack Rabbit *(Lepus californicus)*, White-throated Woodrat *(Neotoma albigula)*, Merriam's Kangaroo Rat *(Dipodomys merriami)*, Little Pocket Mouse *(Perognathus longimembris)*.

Birds: Roadrunner *(Geococcyx californianus)*, Costa's Hummingbird *(Calypte costae)*, Common Raven *(Corvus corax)*, Say's Phoebe *(Sayornis saya)*, Cactus Wren *(Campylorhynchus brunneicapillum)*, LeConte's Thrasher *(Toxostoma lecontei)*, Black-throated Sparrow *(Amphispiza bilineata)*.

Reptiles: Zebra-tailed Lizard *(Callisaurus draconoides)*, Desert Iguana *(Dipsosaurus dorsalis)*, Desert Tortoise *(Gopherus agassizi)*, Coachwhip *(Masticophis flagellum)*.

Invertebrates: Scarred-snout weevils *(Eupagoderes* spp.).

20. DESERT SAND DUNES:

Location and examples:
Sand dunes, large and small, scattered throughout desert areas with plants mostly along dune borders, in dune swales and blow-out pockets. Algodones Dunes east of Holtville, dunes of Central Death Valley, Dunlop Dunes south of Tecopa, Kelso Dunes west of Kelso, scattered dunes such as those in Coachella Valley.

Characteristic plants:
Rice Grass *(Oryzopsis hymenoides)*, Panic Grass *(Panicum urvilleanum)*, Wild Rhubarb *(Rumex hymenosepalus)*, Spanish Needle *(Palafoxia linearis)*, Dune Evening Primrose *(Oenothera deltoides)*, Dune Buckwheat *(Eriogonum deserti)*, (Algodones and nearby dunes only).

Characteristic animals:
Mammals: Kit Fox *(Vulpes velox)*, Desert Kangaroo Rat *(Dipodomys deserti)*.

Birds: Common Raven *(Corvus corax)*.

Reptiles: Zebra-tailed Lizard *(Callisaurus draconoides)*, Coachella Valley Fringe-toed Lizard *(Uma inornata)*, Mojave Fringe-toed Lizard *(U. scoparia)*, Colorado Desert Fringe-toed Lizard *(U. notata)*, Sidewinder *(Crotalus cerastes)*, Western Shovel-nosed Snake *(Chionactis occipitalis)*.

Invertebrates: darkling ground beetles *(Eleodes* spp.), desert ironclad beetles *(Phlaeodes* spp.), a blister beetle *(Phodaga alticeps)*.

21. DESERT WASH:

Location and examples:
Dry sandy water courses leading from canyons of desert mountains; broadening as they near center of basins into which they carry water after torrential or extended rains. Water table usually far beneath surface. Large number of such washes from northern Mojave to Mexican border. Box Canyon Wash, Salton Creek, Arroyo Seco, McCoy Wash, Wingate Wash, Cottonwood Creek.

Characteristic plants:
Colorado Desert washes—Smoke Tree *(Dalea spinosa)*, Desert Ironwood *(Olney tesota)*, Desert Lavender (*Hyptis emoryi)*, Sandpaper Plant *(Petalonyx thurberi)*, Cheese Bush *(Hymenoclea salsola)*, Brandegea *(Brandegea bigelovii)*, Palo Verde *(Cercidium floridum)*, Desert Willow *(Chilopsis linearis)*, Desert Mistletoe *(Phoradendron californica)*.

Mojave Desert washes—Cat's Claw *(Acacia greggii)*, Desert Almond *(Prunus fasciculata)*, Desert Willow *(Chilopsis linearis)*, Bebbia *(Bebbia juncea)*, Wooly Brickellia *(Brickellia incana)*, Hole-in-the-sand Plant *(Nicolletia occidentalis)*.

Characteristic animals:
Mammals: Black-tailed Jack Rabbit *(Lepus californicus)*, Desert Cottontail *(Sylvilagus auduboni)*, White-tailed Antelope Ground Squirrel *(Citellus leucurus)*, Round-tailed Ground Squirrel *(Citellus tereticaudus)*, Desert Wood Rat *(Neotoma lepida)*, Cactus Mouse *(Peromyscus eremicus)*.

Birds: Phainopepla *(Phainopepla nitens)*, Verdin *(Auriparus flaviceps)*, Black-tailed Gnatcatcher *(Poplioptila melanura)*.

Reptiles: Zebra-tailed Lizard *(Callisaurus ventralis)*, Sidewinder *(Crotalus cerastes)*, Desert Tortoise *(Gopherus agassizi)*.

Invertebrates: Wright's Metalmark *(Lephelisca wrighti)*, San Emigdio Blue *(Plebejus emigdionis)*, Mojave Sootywing *(Pholisora libya)*.

22. ALKALI SINK:

Location and examples:
Playas or dry lakes and their borders in desert basins. Many plants salt- or alkali-tolerant, mostly low shrubs.

Characteristic plants:
Saltbush *(Atriplex polycarpa, A. lentiformis, A. hymenolytra),* Inkweed *(Sueda torreyana),* Greasewood *(Sarcobatus vermiculatus),* Iodine Bush *(Allenrolfea occidentalis).*

Characteristic animals:
Mammals: White-tailed Antelope Ground Squirrel *(Citellus leucurus),* Round-tailed Ground Squirrel *(Citellus tereticaudus),* Merriam's Kangaroo Rat *(Dipodomys merriami).*

Birds: Common Raven *(Corvus corax),* Horned Lark *(Eremophila alpestris).*

Reptiles: Zebra-tailed Lizard *(Callisaurus draconoides),* Desert Horned Lizard *(Phynosoma platyrhinos),* Sidewinder *(Crotalus cerastes).*

Invertebrates: Small Blue *(Philotes speciosa),* tiger beetles *(Cicindela* spp.).

23. SALT WATER LAKE:
Location and example:
A single example, Salton Sea, created in Colorado Desert in 1905—1906 by inflow of Colorado River water. Salinity near that of open ocean.

Characteristic plants:
Single-celled algae: diatoms, dinoflagellates, green algae, blue-green algae; Shoal-grass *(Diplanthera wighti)* (introduced but not well established).

Characteristic animals:
Birds: Eared Grebe *(Podiceps caspicus),* White Pelican *(Pelecanus erythrorhynchos),* Gull-billed Tern *(Gelochelidon nilotica).*

Fishes: Sargo *(Anisotremus davidsoni),* Bairdiella *(Bairdiella icistius),* Thread-fin Shad *(Dorosoma petenensis),* Striped Mullet *(Mugil cephalis),* Orange-mouth Corvina *(Cynoscion xanthulus);* Long-jaw Mudsucker *(Gillichthys mirabilis),* Desert Pup-fish *(Cyprinodon macularius),* and Mosquito-fish *(Gambusia affinis)* in shallow water near intake of fresh water from canals or springs.

Invertebrates: Amphipods (most important fish food), a nereid pileworm (also important fish food), protozoans, rotifers, bryozoans, nematodes, copepods, a barnacle *(Balanus amphitrite saltonensis),* larvae of a Salt Fly *(Ephydra gracilis),* and a water boatman *(Trichocorixa* sp.).

24. DESERT CANAL:
Location and examples:
Canals of the irrigated districts of Coachella, Imperial, and Palo Verde valleys.

Characteristic plants:

MacDougal's Cottonwood *(Populus fremontii* var. *mac-dougallii),* Tamarisk *(Tamarix pentandra),* Screwbean Mesquite *(Prosopis pubescens),* Honey Mesquite *(Prosopis glandulosa),* Arrowweed *(Pluchea sericea),* Spiny Aster *(Aster spinosa),* Common Reed *(Phragmites communis),* Common Cat-tail *(Typha latifolia).*

Characteristic animals:

Mammals: Muskrat *(Ondatra zibethica).*

Birds: Mourning Dove *(Zenaidura macroura),* Verdin *(Auriparus flaviceps),* Yellow-headed Blackbird *(Xanthocephalus xanthocephalus),* Abert's Towhee *(Pipilo aberti),* Crissal Thrasher *(Toxostoma dorsale).*

Fishes: Sailfin Molly *(Poecilia latipinna),* Red-sided Shiner *(Notropis lutrensis),* Thread-fin Shad *(Dorosoma petenensis).*

Amphibians: Great Plains Toad *(Bufo cognatus),* Woodhouse's Toad *(Bufo woodhousei),* Bullfrog *(Rana catesbiana).*

Invertebrates: Yuma Skipper *(Ochlodes yuma),* Orange-margined Blue *(Lycaeides melissa),* Asiatic Clam *(Corbicula fluminea).*

25. COLORADO RIVER BOTTOM:

Low areas immediately adjacent to stream flow, a few feet or yards to a third of a mile wide; wider toward delta; moist sandy to clayey soils.

Characteristic plants:

MacDougall's Cottonwood *(Populus fremontii* var. *mac-dougallii),* Black Willow *(Salix goodingii),* Narrow-leaf Willow *(Salix exigua),* Honey Mesquite *(Prosopis juliflora),* Screwbean Mesquite *(Prosopis pubescens),* Arrowweed *(Pluchea sericea),* Quail Brush *(Atriplex lentiformis),* Common Tule *(Scirpus acutus),* Common Cat-Tail *(Typha latifolia).*

Characteristic animals:

Mammals: Beaver *(Castor canadensis),* Raccoon *(Procyon lotor),* Muskrat *(Ondatra zibethica),* Hispid Cotton Rat *(Sigmodon hispidus),* Deer Mouse *(Peromyscus maniculatus).*

Birds: Gambel's Quail *(Lophortyx gambeli),* Ladder-backed Woodpecker *(Dendrocopus scalaris),* Gila Woodpecker *(Centurus uropygialis),* Lucy's Warbler *(Vermivora luciae),* Crissal Thrasher *(Toxostoma dorsale),* Abert's Towhee *(Pipilo aberti),* Song Sparrow *(Melospiza melodia).*

Reptiles: Western Diamondback Rattlesnake *(Crotalus atrox).*

Invertebrates: Viceroy *(Limenitis archippus),* Queen *(Danaus gilippus),* Alpheus Sootywing *(Pholisora alpheus),* a click beetle *(Chalcolepidius tartarius),* cicadas *(Tibicen pruinosa, Diceroprocta apache),* a cicada killer wasp *(Sphecius convallis).*

26. DESERT URBAN:

Location and examples:
Cities and towns of the desert areas, such as Barstow, Indio, El Centro, Niland, Mecca, Palm Springs, Brawley. Plantings very different from those of Pacific coastal areas and, because of climatic conditions, quite restricted.

Characteristic plants:
Cultivated foreign and native trees and shrubs used for ornament and shade. California Fan Palm *(Washingtonia filifera)*, Mexican Fan Palm *(W. gracilis)*, Date Palm *(Phoenix dactylifera)*, Fremont Cottonwood *(Populus fremontii)*, Chinese Elm *(Ulmus parvifolia)*, Oleander *(Nerium oleander)*, Athel *(Tamarix aphylla)*.

Characteristic animals:
Mammals: House Mouse *(Mus musculus)*.

Birds: Barn Owl *(Tyto alba)*, Mourning Dove *(Zenaidura macroura)*, Lesser Nighthawk *(Chordeiles acutipennis)*, House Sparrow *(Passer domesticus)*, House Finch *(Carpodacus mexicanus)*.

Invertebrates: Field Cricket *(Acheta assimilis)*, American Cockroach *(Periplanta americana)*, Singing Katydid *(Neoconocephalus triops)*, House Fly *(Musca domestica)*.

27. DESERT RURAL:

Location and examples:
Flat lands irrigated by wells and canals. Flat lands along the upper Mojave River, Imperial and Coachella valleys, and along the Colorado River.

Characteristic plants:
Alfalfa *(Medicago sativa)*, Grapefruit *(Citrus paradisi)*, Lemon *(Citrus limon)*, Date *(Phoenix dactylifera)*, Grape *(Vitis vinifera)*, Barley *(Hordeum vulgare)*, Lettuce *(Lactuca sativa)*, Sugar Beet *(Beta vulgaris)*, Onion *(Allium cepa)*, Tomato *(Lycopersicon esculentum)*, Cantaloupe *(Cucumis melo* var. *cantalopensis)*. Watermelon *(Citrullus vulgaris)*, Athel *(Tamarix aphylla)*.

Characteristic animals:
Mammals: Coyote *(Canis latrans)*, Black-tailed Jack Rabbit *(Lepus californicus)*.

Birds: Mourning Dove *(Zenaidura macroura)*, Western Kingbird *(Tyrannus verticallis)*, Mockingbird *(Mimus polyglottos)*, Brewer's Blackbird *(Euphagus cyanocephalus)*, Hooded Oriole *(Icterus cucullatus)*.

Reptiles: Gopher Snake *(Pituophis melanoleucus)*, Long-nosed Snake *(Rhinocheilus lecontei)*.

Invertebrates: an eye gnat *(Hippelates collusor)*, White-lined Sphinyx *(Celerio lineata)*, Alfalfa Butterfly *(Colias eurytheme)*.

THE COMMUNITY OF NATURE

In the activities of any community of human beings each member is directly or indirectly dependent on his neighbor. Storekeepers provide food and clothing, lumber dealers supply building materials, city officials arrange for sanitary facilities and police and fire protection. Everyone, whether carpenter, plumber, storekeeper, doctor, or teacher, is a part of a highly organized complex, all living in a state of interdependence: a delicate "balance" has been reached. This balance is not always constant, but gradually or even very suddenly may shift when changes are made by a devastating fire, tornado, or a strike in factory where many men with families work. But adjustments are eventually made, and the community again functions in a normal way in accordance with the new conditions thrust upon it.

It is much the same in communities of animals or plants. The organization is exceedingly complex, often unbelievably so, with each animal or plant affecting in some major or minor way the life of other living beings. If man upsets this balance of nature the results may be devastating to the natural community.

A good example of a food chain is given by Dr. Louis C. Wheeler in his informative book, *Plants and People*. At the beginning of the chain simple, one-celled plants, the diatoms, which live in the cold waters of the Arctic Ocean, manufacture food with the aid of chlorophyll often masked by a golden-brown pigment. The diatoms serve as food for clams, which in turn are eaten by a walrus. An Eskimo eats the walrus, and when the Eskimo dies he is consumed by bacteria. When these perish, there is finally released all the energy first made and stored in the tiny diatoms.

Biological interrelationships in an oak complex

Pyramid of numbers, showing the numbers of animals supported on eighteen square miles of land

In a food chain each link in the chain feeds on the one below it, and in turn is eaten by the one above it. Curiously, the number of links seldom exceeds six. At the bottom of a chain may be the bacteria or microscopic plants such as diatoms, and just a little above them scavenging forms such as amoebae, while at the top are usually the large carnivores. This community organization in nature has variously been called the chain or web of life, the balance of nature, or a biological complex.

For instance, we might speak of the biological complex dependent on a single plant species. On page 58 we see a complex showing some of the different plants and animals that depend directly or indirectly on the oak tree for their existence.

This brings us to another important and interesting concept, the *pyramid of numbers*. At the bottom of the food chain, many animals or plants are involved; at the top, few. It takes an enormous number of diatoms to feed a clam; far fewer in number are the clams that are needed to feed a walrus, still fewer the walruses to feed an Eskimo.

The pyramid of numbers can be illustrated in still another way. For example, on twenty square miles of brush and grassland there will be enough insects and seeds to support about 100,000 white-footed mice and a good many birds. Now the fox is a great mouse-eater, also a minor predator on birds. It has been estimated that the same area will support only 18 to 20 foxes. But the area will supply food for only a single pair of Golden Eagles.

Nature seems to have recognized this arrangement by providing a high capacity to reproduce (biotic potential) for the animals at the bottom of the pyramid, and a low reproductive capacity for those at the apex.

NATURE ACTIVITIES

There are many ways to appreciate nature. For some it is sufficient merely to gaze at the fresh spring beauty of a mariposa lily, to admire a newly-emerged swallowtail butterfly, or to marvel at the kaleidoscopic color reflected from the throat of a hummingbird. For others it will be enough to learn to recognize (by sight or, sometimes, sound) the plants and animals of interest.

We can derive infinite pleasure near at hand, within our own homes, as we explore the world of small things through a microscope and see the attractive form and delicate mechanism of cells, watch the movement of fluids in the vessels of plants and animals, or acquaint ourselves with the marvelous sculpturing of mollusks and seeds.

Still others may wish to give more time and effort to nature study, and for them there is a wealth of varied activities from which to choose. Further information can be obtained from William Hillcourt's *Field Book of Nature Activities* (New York: Putnam, 1950) and Dorothy E. Shuttlesworth's *Exploring Nature with Your Child* (New York: Greystone Press, 1952).

LOOKING AT NATURE

This method of enjoying nature can be just as strenuous or sedentary, expensive or economical, complex or simple as desired. Essentially, looking at nature is what Thoreau did at Walden, Burroughs in New York, and Muir in the High Sierra.

The only equipment necessary for this activity, in its simplest form, is an inquiring mind and sharp eyes. Soon, however, you will want to know the names of the things you see, and for that you will need guidebooks on specific subjects. As you gain experience and perhaps become specialized in your interest, you will want to add special equipment—binoculars for bird watching, a hand lens for insect or plant study, a geologist's hammer, and so on.

One advantage is that you need not go far afield to enjoy this activity. There is much to be seen in your own backyard or in the vacant lot down the street.

Collecting Natural History Specimens

The "pack rat" instinct is strong in most of us, and many people first become interested in nature through carrying an interesting-looking sea shell, rock or pine cone home from a Sunday outing. There is no better way to study certain fields of natural history than by making a collection. If the "rules and regulations" of science are followed, your collection can be not only a source of pleasure to you, but also a storehouse of valuable scientific information.

There is no limit to the variety of objects that can be collected and studied. Some of the specimens commonly collected are butterflies, beetles, and other insects; wildflowers, leaves, pine cones, and wood samples; sea shells and other specimens from beach and tidepool; animal tracks in plaster casts; rocks, minerals, soil samples, and fossils; Indian relics such as arrowheads, stone mortars, and pestles.

Experienced collectors frequently exchange their duplicates. *The Naturalists' Directory* (Box 282, Phillipsburg, New Jersey) lists natural history collectors from all over the world, their subjects of interest, and what they have to exchange.

Collecting Seed Vessels

Dried and mounted in small shallow boxes or on cards of uniform dimensions, seed vessels make an interesting study in form, in manner or arrangement of parts, and in means of efficient seed dispersal. Along with the vessels, mount a few of the seeds. File your cards in a box according to families of plants. The cones of conifers will, of course, require much larger boxes. A botany text will tell you the names of your seed vessels.

Making a Wild Garden

Every home, especially if there are children, should have an area set aside for growing wildflowers, both perennial and annual. The larger the plot the better. Such a garden usually needs little care beyond an occasional weeding in springtime and watering in summer.

Some wildings are readily transplanted when first grown from seeds in pots, but one of the best ways to get them started is to plant the seeds in the open soil. Some seeds will need to be planted within six months after being gathered; others can and should be kept for several years before being planted. Some of the desert plants produce seeds which retain their vitality for many years. Legumes with very hard-coated seeds may need to have their seed coats abraded with a file, dashed in boiling water for a few minutes, or soaked in dilute hydrochloric acid for several hours.

The soil must be prepared so as to afford good drainage. Generally this is accomplished by mixing sand and gravel with our native soils, many of which abound in clay and have minimum amounts of humus. Desert plants, particularly the shrubs, need periods of rest in summer with little or no water.

Bring Them Back Alive

Many of the animals you find in the field are best left right there. In fact, it may be a violation of state game or health laws to capture certain mammals and birds, and it does not make much sense to collect living rattlesnakes unless you are an experienced herptologist and have a good reason for doing so.

However, if you are seriously interested in establishing a home zoo, there are many mammals, reptiles, amphibians, and fishes, as well as a multitude of insects and related creatures, that can supply you with many hours of pleasure both as "zoo keeper" and naturalist-observer. A word of caution: never bring home a living animal of any kind unless you intend to care for it properly or to prepare it immediately as a specimen for your collection. Never bring home plant or animal species that are rare in your area or that are protected by law. Remember that it is against the law to bring in from the wild and keep the Desert Tortoise *(Gopherus agassizi)*. A few suggestions for home zoo projects are:

1. Aquarium—may include tropical or native fishes or tide-pool animals.

2. Terrarium—may contain sand for lizards and snakes or moss for salamanders. Many insects also do well in the terrarium. Doodle bugs (ant lion larvae) are especially interesting to observe in captivity.

3. Ant, termite, and bee colonies do very well in observation nests or hives, and a well-cared-for colony may last for years.

In spring and summer watch for the small fat "crawlers" on trees, shrubs, and herbs, and in flowers. Note their food plants and bring parts of the plants as well as some of the larvae home with you. Place them in jars with dry sand at the bottom, and cover the opening with cheesecloth or a piece of nylon hose held on with a rubber band. After feeding a number of days, the larvae will wrap themselves in a silken coat, attach themselves to a stem, or go under the sand to pupate. Next season it will be interesting to see what emerges. Some will emerge as moths, others as butterflies. If you have adults of the same kind and of different sexes you may watch them mate and soon thereafter see the female laying her eggs, but only on certain plants on which the emerging larvae can feed. Put the eggs under a microscope and make a drawing of them and a description in your notebook. Try to find the name of the food plant and record this too. Butterflies and moths reared in captivity are usually perfect specimens to mount and add to your insect collection.

NATURE UNDER A MICROSCOPE

A binocular microscope, a compound microscope, or a twelve-power hand lens can bring hours of enjoyment. Without instruments of magnification we have no conception of the marvels of form and texture and activity about us. To own a good enlarging instrument should be our first objective. To learn to use it effectively is comparatively simple.

The larger microscopes are mostly for indoor recreation, but the hand lens (with cord attached) should always be carried in the fields or woods to enable us to examine objects minutely and realize the hidden beauty of rocks, the delicate intricacies of flowers, and the details of insect parts to which we

are ordinarily blind. For additional information consult Julian D. Corrington's *Exploring with Your Microscope* (New York: McGraw-Hill, 1957).

WRITING ABOUT NATURE

Nothing clarifies our thinking better than taking
notes on our observations. These can be simply keep-
ing a species list or a list of the kinds of birds or
mammals seen on field trips. Bird watchers note the
names of birds they have seen, with a record of the
date and place. Lists may be made for single field
trips, or one may keep a "life list" over many years
of observation to record each new bird as it is first
seen. A life list is best kept in a special notebook.

Some bird clubs have small printed or mimeo-
graphed lists of local birds for use on field trips.
Check lists for plants, amphibians, reptiles, and mammals of restricted localities are generally supplied by
local nature clubs in the larger communities. You can
make your own check list by copying in a separate
notebook the names obtained in floras and books on
birds, amphibians, and reptiles.

The facts you record in your notebook are the
things you remember. The number of records you
make on each trip is a rather good index of your
progress in natural history education; no notes mean
little progress. Your notes should be not only numerous but detailed. Later these may be helpful and
necessary in preparing a talk or writing an article for
a magazine or scientific journal. If you would like
to know how notes can contribute to literary products
of value, read Donald Culruss Peattie's *An Almanac
for Moderns* (New York: G. P. Putnam, 1935) or Ed-
win Way Teale's *Dune Boy* (New York: Dodd Mead,
1943) and *Circle of the Seasons* (New York: Dodd
Mead, 1953).

Some notetakers write up their observations in the
field. This is a very good way to get down *all* the

important impressions and observations. Others write up their notes each evening or at spare moments during the day. A good rule is never to wait for several days; too many details then slip from memory. Write neatly and with exactness, for the value of your notes depends on legibility and attention to detail. After notes have been taken, consult textbooks to compare your findings with those of competent scholars.

Card records have some advantages over note-books. Notes on cards can be filed according to sub-ject; material of one kind is all together instead of being scattered in different notebooks. Some note-takers write on only one side of the page, then later cut up the pages and file the notes under appropriate headings.

Even though you are an amateur, never undervalue the observations you make. There are many dis-coveries yet to be made to complete the life histories of the most common insects, birds, and other creatures of the field. A student of flies recently found five new and unrecorded species within a mile of his home in spite of the fact that the locality was frequently visited by professional entomologists. The way of bees had been observed for many years, but it was left to K. Von Frisch of Munich to watch their flight habits so carefully, particularly their "dance" on the comb, that he discovered their means of communication with each other concerning their distance and direction from one source of nectar.

An observant student recently collected and worked out for the first time the life histories of sixty moths he found on the grounds of a major university campus, where an active department of entomology had flour-ished for years and where collecting was regularly done.

In preparing a talk or writing an article, there are at least three preparatory steps. First is the rough outline in which we try to arrange our thoughts in logical order. Second, we develop the rough draft to express our ideas in a pleasing manner. Then, as we read and reread this, we find that many refining changes are necessary: we may introduce new note materials, even change the order of sentences and paragraphs; we may leave out material now deemed redundant, or rewrite material to clarify it. Third comes the final draft, neatly typed and ready for delivery before an audience or to be sent to an editor for possible publication.

Most manuscripts need illustrations, and here is where our picture-taking efforts or our skill as a pen or pencil artist is rewarded.

PHOTOGRAPHING NATURE

The camera is the constant companion of the person seeking a knowledge of nature. It need not be expensive; with some of the cheaper models one can obtain very good likenesses of scenes and natural objects.

The most important things to learn, after proper film exposure, are lighting and good composition. The object should be photographed against a background that does not detract but individualizes and prominently sets off the object. Seldom should objects, except in close-up, be in the precise center of the picture. Depth is gained by proper foreground. It is well to have some object such as part of a tree, a small shrub, or rock mass in the foreground and to one side to give perspective.

The photographer who is interested in geology can take pictures illustrating geological phenomena such as evidence of earth slippage, fault lines, contortion of strata, and old shore lines. Insect photography is another interesting hobby for those who have special tripods and lenses allowing close-up work. Satisfactory pictures of birds are best taken by those who can afford telephoto lenses, although excellent shots are sometimes obtained by the amateur with simple equipment.

The objective is to accumulate enough photos of one subject to make adequate comparative studies. These may be mounted in an album of birds or of flowers, or of some other subject. It is well to specialize in the type of material and not photograph at random. Helpful and interesting references are Allan D. Cruickshank's *Hunting with the Camera* (New York: Greenberg, 1956), and Edward S. Ross' *Insects Close Up* (Berkeley: University of California Press, 1953). For the latest information on nature photography, see the articles in photography and nature magazines, and various booklets by the Eastman Kodak Company.

WATCHING AND PHOTOGRAPHING CLOUDS

You can derive much pleasure from photographing different types of clouds and beautiful sunrises and sunsets. If you will, with the aid of a book, classify the clouds you can then mount the pictures in a "cloud book." Such an exercise can teach you much about clouds and their relation to different kinds of weather. It is surprising how many kinds of cloud pictures can be taken in a single year. Helpful books include Glen T. Trewartha's *An Introduction to Climate* (New York: McGraw-Hill, 1954), chapter 3;

Arthur N. Strahler's *Physical Geography* (New York: Wiley, 1960), chapter 10; and Sverre Petterssen's *Introduction to Meteorology* (New York: McGraw-Hill, 1958) chapter 2.

SKETCHING NATURE

As you sit by the trail and observe chipmunks at work and play, you may wish to capture their characteristic appearance with a pencil. A small sketching pad will fit in your field kit or pocket. Although your sketches may never have the look of a professional wildlife artist's drawing, they will improve with practice and enhance the value of your notes. Birds, mammals, insects, flowers, and trees are all likely subjects. You may also want to prepare a vegetation map of a habitat or a sketch of the habitual routes taken by various birds, bees, or butterflies as they go about their daily activities.

To help you get started, take a drawing course at the local adult evening school, YWCA, or YMCA, or consult a book on sketching. Good books on nature drawing include Frances Zweifel's *A Handbook of Biological Illustration* (Chicago: University of Chicago Press, 1961), Frederic Sweeney's *Course in Drawing and Painting Birds* (New York: Reinhold, 1961), Henry C. Pitz' *Drawing Trees* (New York: Watson-Guptill, 1956), Frederic Sweeney's *Techniques of Drawing and Painting Wildlife* (New York: Reinhold, 1959), and Charles S. Papp's *Scientific Illustration: Theory and Practice* (Dubuque, Iowa: Wm. C. Brown Co., 1968).

NATURE AT NIGHT

At first thought, the study of nature might seem to be strictly a daytime activity (except for stargazing), but it is obvious that the plants and animals are also present at night and that many animals are far more active after dark. Some college courses include a twenty-four-hour field trip so that the varied activities of nature can be observed in one place throughout a full day and night.

Many mammals, amphibians, and insects, as well as some reptiles and birds, can best be observed during darkness. The call notes of owls, nighthawks, and frogs may make the evening interesting, and the pre-dawn chorus of songbirds in the spring offers a concert that, once experienced, is never forgotten.

Many animals can be identified at night by their "eye shine." If you attach a miner's lantern to your head or hold a flashlight near your eyes but pointed ahead along the trail, you will be surprised at the number of animals encountered on a nocturnal hike through the woods and across the fields.

For more information on nature at night, see Lorus J. and Margery J. Milne's *The World of Night* (New York: Harper, 1956).

CAMPFIRES

Gasoline and gas-fuel stoves inside house-campers have unfortunately largely taken the place of the traditional campfire. In most mountain wooded areas, fires, except in "prepared" stoves at designated campgrounds, are forbidden throughout much of the year; so it is left to the desert camper to enjoy his natural fire and the pleasing odors that arise from the burning of native woods. Small fires at any time are the most serviceable both for warmth and for cooking. Hard woods are preferred, since they yield the hottest flames and the least smoke; moreover, these woods leave the best beds of hot glowing coals on which we can gaze during those thought-provoking moments before we retire for the night.

The good camper knows with accuracy the names of the wood he burns. If possible, he uses a different kind of wood for each campfire, and thus learns their burning qualities, the characteristic colors of their flames, and the distinctive odors of their smoke.

The Sounds of Nature

No music is more satisfying than the vibrant songs of birds, the stridulation of katydids, of crickets and certain grasshoppers, the drone of flies or bees, and the piping notes of frogs and toads. Edward A. Armstrong's *A Study of Bird Song* (Oxford University Press, 1963) is helpful to those seriously interested in the music of birds. The record, *Music in Nature*, by Dr. Loye Miller (sold by the Cooper Ornithological Society, Department of Zoology, University of California, Los Angeles 90025), shows how we can develop the ability to enjoy and identify the sounds in our environment. Many records of bird songs and the sounds of amphibians, fishes, insects, and other animals are available from the National Audubon Society (see page 98).

Nature Games and Plays

A popular nature activity, particularly with young children, is the playing of games based on common plants, animals, and rocks. These can be as simple as a modification of the old favorite, "I Spy," or as elaborate as a one-act play. Nature games can be played by any number in almost any situation, indoors or outdoors. Games using nature materials and plays with nature or conservation themes can provide added interest for school and/or camp programs.

For example, an interesting game may be based on the fascinating odors of nature. There are hundreds of distinctive leaf odors, some very pleasing, such as those from the crushed leaves of the mints, some of the psoraleas, conifers, willows, and sycamores. Others are not so pleasing, but are valuable guides to identification. Odors are as diagnostic for many plants as the appearance of their leaves and flowers.

To play the "smelling game," have someone who is familiar with these odors present the crushed leaves or the flowers to the nostrils of the blindfolded players.

Children like to see how good a score they can make, and soon become expert.

ANIMAL TRACKS

Animals, particularly those which travel over sand or dusty roads and footpaths, leave evidence of their wanderings in their footprints.

With dry powdered plaster of Paris, water, a spoon, and a vessel in which to make a thick gravy-like mixture, a permanent plaster-cast record can be made of animal tracks. See Olaus Murie's *A Field Guide to Animal Tracks* (Boston: Houghton Mifflin Co., 1954). The same results may be achieved by spraying the tracks with acrylic spray, Krylon, or clear lacquer. These sprays soon harden and cement the sand or dust particles; the track, with its sand or dust base, can then be lifted out and carried home in cardboard box. The latter procedure is often the most satisfactory because it is quickest and does not require making a positive from the mold, as does the plaster-of-Paris method.

An interesting game when walking over sand dunes (they are often "alive" with tracks) is to see who is best at identifying the track makers. *A Field Guide to Animal Tracks* (see above) one of the *Peterson Field Guide Series*, contains a mine of information about mammals and is a book to be carried in the field knapsack or auto. Unfortunately, there is no similar book on the tracks of insects and other arthropods, nor on the tracks of birds. Here is an opportunity for someone to write such a book.

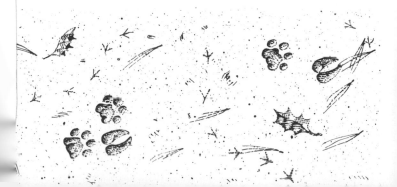

Exploring Streams

Walking along streams or streamlets, even exploring dry desert washes, can be an interesting pastime, for there are all sorts of things to see in the water, in rock crannies, and along the banks—things you never see anywhere else. Keep notes on the day's rambles; this is a good way to realize the richness of life of a special environment. The variety of small life, from snails to water-loving insects and water spiders, stream-side grasses, sedges, and ferns, will amaze you.

Try to trace a stream to its source, which may be a lake, a pond, or a spring in a hillside meadow. Mountain streams are particularly interesting. Keep alert, as rattlesnakes, during spring, summer, and early autumn, often lie coiled on rocks at the streamside, ready to strike their prey, such as small mammals and birds.

Beachcombing

For a hobby that combines exercise and fun, beachcombing is hard to beat. It is especially rewarding just after a storm, when interesting natural treasures such as sea shells and driftwood are washed ashore.

Skin and Scuba Diving

The nature hobby that has had the most phenomenal growth in recent years is probably skin and scuba diving. Many divers are interested only in the sport and adventure, but diving also provides a wonderful opportunity to learn much about a little-known subject—plant and animal life underwater.

Exploring Caves

Southern California has comparatively few caves. In spite of rather extensive limestone formations on the north face of the San Bernardino Mountains, no caves of importance have yet been discovered there.

Perhaps the only caverns of interest to the speleologist are the partially explored Mitchell's Caverns of the Providence Mountains in eastern San Bernardino County. This high desert area is now a state park; its Mary Beal Nature Trail is of botanical interest. A small admission fee is charged and guides are provided. These caverns are in limestone of Lower Permian Age. To reach them, turn off Highway 66 at Essex and drive northward 22 miles.

Some shallow caves occur in the extensive lava beds about a mile east of Pisgah Crater in San Bernardino County west of Amboy. They are difficult to find unless one has a guide familiar with the area. A road leading south from Highway 66 leads to Pisgah Crater, where cinder has been mined.

Newberry Caves (Smith and Shiuling caves) south of Newberry in San Bernardino County were once homes of prehistoric man. Some interesting archaeological material taken from this site can be seen at the San Bernardino County Museum at Bloomington, California.

Interpreting the Face of the Earth

With a knowledge of physiography, a ride through or flight over the mountains and valleys of southern California can be more meaningful and enjoyable. By learning the proper signs, you can locate earthquake fault lines, long-extinct volcanic cones, or determine that certain mountain peaks were once at the bottom of the sea.

Rock Collecting

The rock-collecting hobby intelligently pursued may yield much pleasure for lovers of nature. Southern California with its many colorful rock surfaces, not too heavily masked by plant cover, offers unusual opportunities for the rock collector to build up his

cabinet of interesting rocks and gemstones. The numerous clubs for amateur mineral collectors are willing to help beginners, and usually conduct field trips to interesting localities. It is commendable that these clubs do not leave a collecting area in shambles, but teach their members to select only what is needed to make their specimen drawers complete.

Many rock enthusiasts have cutting and polishing equipment which can reveal the rare inner beauty of specimens. A good book to consult is by Vinson Brown and David Allen; *Rocks and Minerals of California and Their Stories* (Healdsburg: Naturegraph Co., 3d rev. ed., 1965).

COLLECTING FOSSILS

Important fossil-collecting sites for those interested in the tiny protozoans, so beautiful under the microscope and so important to oil prospectors, are found in Los Angeles City, at Newport Lagoon, Silverado Canyon, Capistrano Beach, and in the Palos Verdes Hills. Remember that collecting is not permitted in most parks, and on private property only with the permission of the owner.

Unknown to many, southern California has great thicknesses of rock filled with the remains of invertebrate animals and astonishing numbers of marine fish, birds, and mammals. Those who are interested in fossil-bearing rocks will do well to read *Geology of California*, Bulletin 170, chapter 3, "Historical

Geology," published by the Division of Mines, Department of Natural Resources, State of California, in 1954.

The following are important fossil sites. The animal remains found there are listed:

Santa Barbara County: *Tick Canyon,* east of Santa Barbara—pocket mice, rabbits, oreodonts, browsing hares, hawk. *Tecuija beds,* east of Santa Barbara—paired-horn rhinoceros, "deerlet," bear-dog, tree sqirrel.

Ventura County: *Sespe area*—five genera of primitive rodents, three genera of primitive carnivores, primitive insectivores, early lemur monkey, hedgehog, large cat, field mice, rabbit, early saber-toothed cat.

Los Angeles County: in Hancock Park on north side of Wilshire Boulevard, near Fairfax Avenue, Los Angeles, *Rancho La Brea,* famous "tar traps"—the plant record poor, but an unusual number of fossils of living birds (47) and mammals (21) besides at least five extinct birds and eleven extinct mammals. (Los Angeles County Museum handbook, *Rancho La Brea* describes this world-famous locality.) *Mint Canyon,* once characteristic Oak-Woodland, Chaparral, Grassland community—mastodons, dogs, rhinos, peccaries, rabbit, camels, pronghorns.

Kern County: *Ricardo beds,* Grassland-Woodlands community—cats, dogs, rhinos, peccaries, rabbits, camels, pronghorn, weasels, oreodonts, long-jawed mastodons.

Riverside County: *Bautista Canyon*—a large, true horse, true deer, rabbits, ground sloth, camels, tapirs, pronghorns. *Mount Eden*—break-jawed mastodons, dogs, cats, bears, peccaries, ground sloths, camels, raccoons, wolverines, amphibious rhinoceros. *San Timeteo Canyon*—giant land tortoises, camels, ground sloths, true deer.

San Bernardino County: *Barstow formation*—large and small browsing horses, pronghorns, peccaries, chipmunks, pocket mice, rabbits, oreodonts, dogs, hyenoid dogs, saber-toothed cats, true cats, camels, shrews, birds, tortoises, fresh-water mollusks. *Lake Manix beds,* eastern Mojave Desert—unusual assortment of mammals; *Avawatz Mountains,* near south end of Death Valley—fauna similar to types of Ricardo Formation in Kern County.

Inyo County: *Coso Mountains,* abundant grasslands region—hyenoid dogs, short-jawed mastodons, meadow mice, large peccary. *Titus Canyon formation,* wooded savanna region, Grapevine Mountains of Death Valley Region—rodents, dogs, brontotheres, rhinos, tapirs, credonts, camelids, deerlets.

COLLECTING BOOKS AND READING ABOUT NATURE

Every home should contain a well-selected, well-rounded nature library which is easily accessible.

Handbooks such as the *Peterson Field Guide Series* should form the core of the library. To these should be added several general works on natural history such as the *Standard Natural History,* edited by W. P. Pycraft (London and New York: Frederick Warne & Co., Ltd., 1931), and a number of books and pamphlets dealing with local flora and fauna. Many of these are listed among the Suggested References on page 100.

Educational institutions of higher learning such as Stanford University and the University of California publish books and periodicals dealing with the natural history of the state. Lists of such publications can be obtained directly from their presses (University of California Press, Berkeley; Stanford University Press, Stanford). Local museums issue pamphlets or booklets which can be purchased from them. Second-hand book dealers, both in the United States and in England, publish valuable catalogues of natural history publications both old and recent (Foyles, 119-125

Charing Cross Road, London W. C. 2; Heffer and Sons, Ltd., Petty Curry, Cambridge; James Thin, 53-59 South Bridge, Edinburgh; Pierce Book Co., Winthrop, Iowa; Eric Lundberg, Ashton, Maryland; Henry Tripp, 92-06 Jamaica Avenue, Woodhaven, New York). Your local libraries can give you addresses of other dealers listing nature books.

It is fascinating to visit second-hand bookstores, Salvation Army stores, and others, where you may find used nature books, often hard-to-get ones, at reasonable prices. Their selections are continually changing; so it is good practice to visit such bookstores several times a year. The largest stores are in the cities, such as Los Angeles, Long Beach, and San Diego, but some of the best bargains are often found in the small shops of the smaller towns.

LETTER WRITING

Writing letters describing your experiences, travels, and observations of nature are welcomed by your friends. Why not seek a few "pen pals," preferably in remote places, who share your interests and would enjoy an exchange of ideas through correspondence? Enclose drawings you have made and snapshots you have taken. Southern California, with its distinctive plants and animals of the mountains and deserts, offers a wealth of material which, if skillfully described, will fascinate your correspondents in any part of the world. Names and addresses of persons interested in such correspondence may be found in various hobby magazines and in *The Naturalists Directory*. (See page 62.)

NATURE CLUBS

By joining a natural history club you can exchange information with others as well as gain inspiration from them. Most of the larger centers of population have Audubon societies, herpetological clubs, shell clubs, or horticultural or botanical societies. If there is no nature club in your community, you might organize one from a nucleus of your nature-loving friends, even if there are only three or four to start with. Meeting in the homes, you can bring specimens and pictures to discuss; also, you can invite someone well versed in natural history to talk to the group and lead them on a field trip. If there is a natural history museum anywhere near, its director can supply the names of organizations with which you can affiliate and thus help to make your own club meetings more interesting and profitable.

SEEING NATURE IN SOUTHERN CALIFORNIA

Enjoyment of the outdoor world can take many forms. Some nature devotees concentrate on bird watching. Others study plants; and still others find their greatest enjoyment in strolling along the beaches to pick up shells.

In the pages which follow are described many places and ways to see and enjoy nature in southern California. Sharp eyes and an inquiring mind are the most essential tools. Books, binoculars, hand lenses, microscopes, cameras, and a geologist's pick are all useful in their place, but many important discoveries have been made without them.

You need not go far afield on walks or drives to see worthwhile things in nature. Often it is in your garden or along the parkway of a city street that absorbing and stimulating objects may be observed. Many, however, wish to venture farther afield, to explore the inexhaustible sources of beauty in mountains, seashore, and deserts. Such rambles are usually more enjoyable when shared by a friend or a group having similar interests. Nature trips are conducted by Audubon societies and other nature clubs.

A few basic rules should be observed so that our activities do not impinge on the rights of others or destroy natural beauty for future generations to enjoy.

1. Do not pick flowers or remove plants growing along highways or footpaths. Leave them for others to enjoy. Remember that plants help to hide the litter thrown out by thoughtless motorists.

2. Do not collect plants, animals, or mineral specimens in county, state, or national parks.

3. Do not throw litter of any kind, even gum wrappers, from your car window. The same precaution should be observed along foot trails. Never throw trash, including fish cleanings, into ponds, lakes, or streams.

4. Never break glass bottles or jars by throwing them against rocks or shooting at them for sport. Glass never decays. Splinters and larger pieces of glass with their sharp cutting edges are a hazard to wild animals and to persons coming in contact with them. Many an attractive-looking rock surface has been ruined for others to look at because of scattered glass left by bottle shooters.

5. Always obtain permission before entering private property and thank the owner for the privilege of studying wilderness ways on his land. To collect specimens, ask the owner's permission. It is very important not to damage gates and fences, trample

crops, help yourself to fruits and vegetables, or disturb livestock. No litter of any kind should be left behind; cast-off paper plates and cups, cans, and the remains of your lunch should be taken home or placed in roadside trash receptacles.

6. If logs or stones have been overturned, replace them so that wildlife communities will not be disrupted. If large holes have been dug to get specimens, refill them to avoid injury to domestic animals.

7. Never take more specimens than you have use for, especially if the animals, plants, or minerals are rare. It is then best not to collect any, but to learn about the species by observing them in a museum, zoological garden, park, or private collection.

8. Be exceedingly careful with matches and fires. The good camper makes a very small fire, which he never leaves until it is completely extinguished; moreover, he tries to learn the names of the woods he burns.

9. First-aid knowledge gained by attending a Red Cross class or reading a Scout Handbook or Red Cross Manual is essential. A simple light-weight first-aid kit, including materials for the treatment of rattlesnake bite should always be carried.

10. When you leave home or camp always tell some responsible person where you plan to go and approximately when you expect to return.

11. If you are venturing into rough, heavily wooded, or unfamiliar areas, carry a lunch, a canteen of water, matches, notebook and pencil, and a good topographic map showing physical details of the area and a source of water. Do not leave the trails.

A companion who has had experience in wild country can be a great help; and if he knows the plants and animals he can be a source of inspiration and pleasure.

MAPS

Maps which you can use to plan field trips and camping trips are published by the Automobile Club of Southern California and the National Automobile Club. Many of them cover very local areas and are supplied free to club members. The United States Forest Service maps, showing details of forested areas, may be obtained from the forest supervisor of each forest or from local rangers. The United States Geological Survey publishes detailed contour maps of almost every area in southern California. Such maps are particularly helpful to those exploring our wild-lands on foot. They may be purchased from the U. S. Geological Survey, Denver, Colorado. The office supplies free of charge a guide map showing the areas covered and the maps that are available. All the major oil companies publish very good road maps indicating not only the major highways but lesser roads leading to out-of-the-way places of special interest to the naturalist. They may be obtained at most service stations.

SCENIC DRIVES AND FIELD TRIPS

If early and adequate rains come, southern California's winters and springs may bring wonderful displays of wild-flowering annuals and perennial shrubs in unplowed fields, in disturbed soil bordering roads, and in wastelands of hills and lower mountainsides. Walks abroad with wild-flower book in hand are rewarding indeed. Also yielding much pleasure are automobile trips to the back country where wilderness still survives.

The following suggested journeys will take you to places where in season wildflowers are usually plentiful:

1. Riverside to San Diego on Highway 395 with diversions to Fallbrook, Lilac, and Ramona; return by way of Warners Hot Springs and Hemet on Highway 79. Wild lilacs (*Ceanothus* spp.), beautiful oaks (*Quercus agrifolia* and *Q. engelmannii*), Red-shank (*Adenostoma sparsifolium*), *Xylococcus bicolor*, and several kinds of manzanita.

Wild lilacs are especially colorful in late February, March, and April.

2. From Hemet up through Bautista Canyon (earth road) on to Anza thence over Pines-to-Palms Highway (74) to Palm Desert. Large manzanitas, Parry Piñon (Nut-pine), One Leaf Piñon, Agave, Ocotillo, Wild Apricot, and Red-shank prominent along the way.

3. Santa Paula to Ojai, then to Carpinteria using Highway 150, Highway 399, and a byway through Casitas Pass. A good area in which to become acquainted with chaparral and coastal scrub, Toyon *(Heteromeles arbutifolia)* in July, Heart-leaf Penstemon *(Penstemon cordifolius)* in June and July, White Lilac *(Ceanothus megacarpus)*, Spiny Wild Lilac *(Ceanothus spinosus)*, White-leaf Sage *(Salvia leucophylla)* in June and July, Bush Monkey Flower *(Diplacus longiflorus)* in May, Owl's Clover *(Orthocarpus purpurascens)* in April.

4. From Corona over Santa Ana Mountains by way of Tin Mine Canyon, Oak Flats, and Black Star Canyon on a rather steep earth-surfaced road which may be closed from April to November. Make local inquiry. Leads through fine chaparral country.

5. Santa Inez Mountains, crossed by several black-topped roads leading to Coast Highway 101. Go from Santa Barbara to Lompoc on Highway 150, then on Highway 1 to junction with 101, then back to Santa Barbara. These mountains, most northerly of east-west trending ranges of southern Caifornia, are of special interest to geologists but also appeal to botanists and bird lovers.

6. Santa Monica Mountains. Several roads lead between Highway 101 and 101 Alternate. Diversified plant cover; many live oaks. Ribbonwood *(Adenostoma sparsifolium)*, common in eastern San Diego County and southern middle Riverside County, has a small outpost here.

7. Mecca to Box Canyon by way of Highway 195 to junction with Highway 60 and 70, then through Joshua Tree National Monument to Twentynine Palms. Scenic desert route through eroded clay and sandstone hills to fields of Bigelow's Cholla and Joshua Tree forests. Return to Highway 99 and go west to Banning.

8. From San Bernardino to Victorville on Highway 66, thence on Highway 18 to Lucerne Valley. Take paved road northward to Barstow. Return by way of old Route 66 to Victorville. This route, following partway along Mojave River, affords a good sample of typical Mojave Desert country, with Creosote Bush, the Joshua Tree, and Cottonwood thickets along river. Wild flowering annuals usually best in April.

9. San Diego to La Mesa by Highway 80. From La Mesa to Campo on Highway 94, then north to junction with Highway 80. At Descanso go north on Highway 79 to Julian and Santa Isabel. Turn west on Highway 78 to Escondido and back to San Diego on Highway 395. Chaparral, live oaks *(Quercus agrifolia, Q. engelmanii),* and superb mountain scenery, pine forest, and streamside trees.

10. Redlands to Big Bear Lake via City Creek and Running Springs on Highway 30. From Big Bear Lake a new scenic highway leads to Barton Flats and Mill Creek, then back to Redlands. Many kinds of mountain plant and animal communities and mountain trees: Big-cone Spruce, California Black Oak, White Fir, Sugar Pine, Western Yellow Pine, etc. Highly recommended at any time of year. At higher elevations (7,000–8,000 ft.) snow may be found during winter.

MOUNTAINS TO CLIMB

San Gorgonio Peak (elevation 11,502 ft) can be ascended from the south or north side; the south climb is the easier. This is the highest mountain in southern California; it affords an unexcelled view of much of our desert wasteland. Snow usually lies on the north face until July. It is an eerie experience to spend a summer night on the summit, listen to the unruly winds, and watch the sun rise over the mountains of distant Arizona. Relict plants at the highest elevation include *Draba corrugata, Potentilla wheeleri,* a dwarf locoweed *(Oxytropis oreophila),* and *Phyllodoce breweri* with rose-colored bowl-shaped corolla. On Fish Creek (7,000–7,600 ft.) are the only colonies of Quaking Aspen *(Populus tremuloides)* in southern California. This tree occurs in the Sierra San Pedro Martir in Lower California. Among birds to be seen in groves of Lodgepole Pine and Limber Pine near the mountain top are Clark's Nutcracker, Townsend's Solitaire, Cassin's Finch, Brown Creeper, and Oregon Juneo.

*San Jacinto Peak** (elevation 10,831 ft.), in San Jacinto Wilderness State Park. The 9½-mile trail from Idyllwild to the summit is a not-too-difficult climb in good weather. Foot trails lead through fine Transition Zone and Boreal Zone forests. At Round Valley and vicinity, Lodgepole Pine is seen as well as thickets of Chinquapin or Dwarf Chestnut *(Castanopsis sempervirens)* and Deer-brush or Snow-brush *(Ceanothus cordulatus)*. In the upper Transition and Boreal forests you may see Clark's nutcracker and the Lodgepole Chipmunk, and perhaps, above the peak, the Golden Eagle.

San Antonio Peak or Mount Baldy (elevation 10,080 ft.). The granite rocks have been subjected to unusual pressure so that they break up into "flakes" rather than angular or rounded blocks. A few Piñon Pines are seen on the south side of the mountain in Cattle Canyon, and Western Juniper on the southeast side above San Antonio Falls (only locality other than San Bernardino Mountains in southern California). Lodgepole Pine grows near the summit.

Sugar Loaf (elevation 9,842 ft.). Ascending the north face of this rounded-top mountain, you pass through Upper Sonoran, Lower and Upper Transition, and Boreal Zones. Lodgepole Pine is found near the top. At the north base of the mountain is a large sagebrush flat and extensive thickets of Western Serviceberry *(Amelanchier alnifolia)* whose ripe fruit attracts many birds. The spring on the north side, in a deep canyon at 8,500 feet, is a good place to study birds. Dr. Joseph Grinnell once counted fifteen species there between 10 and 11 A.M.

Mount Pinos (elevation 8,831 ft.), Ventura County. There is a road up the northeast side. The best climb is from the north side. There are forests of Jeffrey Pine, White Fir, California Black Oak, at least two

----
* The 8516 foot level may also be reached from Chino Canyon by the Palm Springs Aerial Tramway.

species of manzanita, large flats of *Iris missouriensis,* and the dull lavendar Mariposa Lily *(Calochortus invenustus)* in season.

Frasier Mountain (elevation 8,026 ft.) Ventura County. A road leads to a forest lookout at the top. Look for *Ceanothus cordulatus, Wyethia ovata,* and the usual Transition Zone trees.

Clark Mountain (elevation 7,903 ft.), eastern San Bernardino County. This isolated limestone peak is best approached from the northside; there are no trails. Near the summit is a valley filled with White Fir, California Juniper, and One-Leaf Piñon Pine *(Pinus monophylla).* This is the type locality of several rare plants and a land snail, all found near the summit. Small century plants *(Agave utahensis* var. *nevadensis)* from thickets on lower slopes. The flora is much like that of higher mountains to the north.

Kingston Peak (elevation 7,320 ft.), northeastern San Bernardino County. There are no trails; climbers usually start from a high point on the road which crosses its northern flank. Near the summit are found *Nolina parryi* and White Fir. Winter, spring, and autumn are the best seasons.

Telescope Peak (elevation 11,049 ft.), the highest point in the Panamint Mountains, is reached by way of Wild Rose Canyon to Mahogany Flats (elevation 8,133 ft.) thence by trail of 7 miles. The view of the surrounding desert, especially of Death Valley, is remarkable. There is snow in winter. This mountain is of recent vigorous uplift, with an extremely abrupt west front. Mountain Mahogany, One-Leaf Piñon Pine, and California Juniper are found up to 9,000 feet, and Bristle-cone Pine and Limber Pine near the summit.

Cucamonga Peak (elevation 8,859 ft.). This high summit of the San Gabriel Range is composed of a series of faulted blocks which were elevated to their present position during Pleistocene times. There are several trails to the summit. On this mountain are well-protected bands of Bighorn Sheep. Big-cone Spruce grows at lower elevations, White Fir and Ponderosa Pine farther up, and Lodgepole Pine at the summit.

Cuyamaca Peak (elevation 6,515 ft.). From the top you can enjoy a commanding view of San Diego County and areas far to the south in Lower California; El Providencia in the Sierra San Pedro Martir can be seen when it is covered with snow. A large fire scar mars the conical peak on its west side. Here are found Sonoma Sage *(Salvia sonomensis)*, also known from the Santa Lucia Mountains near Monterey, and Azalea *(Azalea occidentalis)*, which occurs in the San Gabriel and San Jacinto mountains but not in the San Bernardinos. Look for rare Stephenson's Cypress *(Cupressus stephensonii)* at the head of King Creek.

FRESH-WATER AND SALT LAKES

In the southern California fresh-water lakes (natural and artificial), listed below, aquatic life studies are possible. Some of these bodies of water are open to public use; others are accessible only by permit. Local inquiry must be made.

Santa Barbara County: *Cachuma Lake,* about 25 miles northwest of Santa Barbara on Highway 150 Used mostly by fishermen and boaters.

Ventura County: *Lake Sherwood,* reached by Highways 101 and 27. *Malibu Lake* and *Lake Enchanto,* reached by Highway 101 and short drive southward. *Lake McGrath,* north of Oxnard.

Los Angeles County: *Elizabeth Lake,* north of Saugus. *Bouquet Canyon Lake,* between Palmdale and Saugus.

San Bernardino County: *Big Bear Lake,* on Highway 18, in San Bernardino Mountains northeast of Redlands. Yellow

Pine and Western Juniper Forest. Used primarily by fisherman and water skiers. Supplies irrigation for fruit growers in San Bernardino Valley. *Lake Arrowhead,* reached by Highway 18. Rather large artificial lake, bordered by pine forest. Used by water sportsmen and fishermen. *Lake Gregory,* reached by Highway 18 and short drive (2.2 miles) northeastward. Small artificial lake used by fishermen, boat enthusiasts, and bathers. *Lake Havasu,* on Colorado River between Needles and Parker Dam, reached by Highway 95, thence by road north. Marvelously scenic. Beautiful autumn and winter camping, boating, fishing.

Riverside County: *Lake Hemet,* reached by Highway 74. In Western Yellow Pine country. Much used by fishermen. *Lake Elsinore,* reached by Highway 71 form Corona or Highway 74 from Perris or San Juan Capistrano. Used mostly by water sportsmen. Water alkaline because of dissolved salts. *Salton Sea,* unique inland lake of saline water in bottom of Colorado Desert partly in Riverside County, partly in Imperial County. Largest body of inland water in the state, covering about 340 square miles: 30 miles long and 12 miles wide at widest part. Surface elevation about 235 feet below sea level. Fishing, boating, water skiing, camping, and picknicking year-round in Salton Sea State Park. Best seasons autumn and winter; spring months likely to be windy. For animals and plants inhabiting its saline waters see p. 54. Consult *Ecology of the Salton Sea; California in Relation to Sportfishery,* Fish Bulletin No. 113, California Department of Fish and Game, 1961, for details of natural history.

Imperial County: *Laguna and Imperial reservoirs,* north of Yuma, Arizona, on Colorado River, reached by Highway 80 and a short road northward. Used primarily for recreation and irrigation.

DRY LAKES

Dry lakes are flat barren areas at the bottom of undrained desert basins where water, carrying silt and salts, temporarily accumulates after heavy rains and flash floods. The water, seldom more than a foot or two deep, soon dries up, leaving a layer of salt-filled clay or a glistening white salt deposit which can be seen many miles away. Dry lakes are plentiful on the Mojave Desert and the deserts of adjacent Nevada; there are 62 dry lakes on the Mojave Desert alone. Some are rough-surfaced and spongy (wet type), with water table just under the surface; others (dry type) are hard-surfaced and smooth, and there is little chance of finding water beneath, even by deep drilling.

Some of these dry lakes have been far more extensive in the past. Their former size may be roughly estimated by the areas of gray-green Saltbush *(Atriplex)* and other halophytic (salt-tolerant) plants along their present borders. Beyond lies a zone of green Creosote Bush. In Pleistocene times, some now-dry lake beds were covered for long periods with fresh water in which fishes and mollusks lived. This food source attracted aboriginal peoples, and we still find the evidence of their encampments in the form of clamshells, broken pottery, and wood ashes from their campfires.

You might enjoy camping on the edge of a dry lake to investigate the strange plants and search for Indian artifacts. Dry fuel is usually plentiful; and at night the flames of your campfire will be beautifully tinted yellow, green, blue, purple, and red, owing to the presence of different salts that the plants have stored in their woody tissues.

Many dry lakes have no access roads and can be reached only in a 4-wheel-drive vehicle capable of going through sand. Caution is necessary, for just below the apparently dry surface may lie wet slippery clay, dangerous because your car may suddenly sink and become mired in it.

SAND DUNE AREAS

Because of their clean, soft surface and beautiful contours, sand dunes are fascinating to visit. Since the winds are constantly shifting the fine sands, footprints are soon effaced. The best time to visit dunes is during calm sunny days in October, November, and

December. Many spring days are good times to explore them too, especially if wildflowers are blooming along the dune borders and in the protected blowouts: sand verbenas (*Abronia* spp.), Dune Evening Primrose (*Oenothera trichocalyx*), Wild Rhubarb (*Rumex hymenosepalus*), Croton (*Croton californica*), and many other sand-loving plants. Expect to see sand-diving lizards of the genus *Uma*, big black darkling beetles (*Eleodes*), and the small round-backed oval sand beetles (*Eusattus muricata*) with yellow band of short closely set hairs across the thorax; the latter are especially abundant after rains. Trails of other ground-dwelling insects, small mammals, lizards and snakes are abundant along dune borders. This is a good place to study animal tracks.

The principal sand-dune areas are as follows:

Algodones Dunes, east of El Centro in Imperial County. Low dunes about 40 miles long and 2 to 6 miles wide. Highway 80 passes over them. Crests or some rise 200 to 300 feet.

Amargosa or Dunlap Dunes, about 30 miles north of Baker, near Amargosa River bend, reached by a side road leading east from Highway 127.

Barchan Dunes, west of Salton Sea, Riverside County, series of disconnected small, low crescent- or hoof-shaped dunes, some east, some west of Highway 99.

Cadiz Dunes, between Cadiz Dry Lake and Kilbeck Mountains in eastern San Bernardino County. Nearest Highway 66.

Death Valley Dunes, in center of valley. Picturesque low sand formations near Stovepipe Wells.

Eureka Valley Dunes, western and southern end of valley, Inyo County. An improved road leads from Big Pine across a hip of Last Chance Mountains into northern end of Death Valley.

Kelso Dunes, south of Union Pacific R.R., southwest of Kelso. A road from Kelso to Amboy in San Bernardino County passes near them. Highest dunes in California.

Midland Dunes, between Midland Station and Riverside Mountain, Riverside County; on road between Rice and Blythe.

A belt of dunes, adjacent to Pacific Ocean, Santa Barbara and Ventura counties. Other small dunes along coast southward to San Diego. Interesting because of their specialized flora. Portions may be closed by the military.

PARKS AND CAMPGROUNDS

Public campgrounds and picnic areas are especially good as bases for walking excursions into surrounding scenic areas. Below are listed some of the larger and best known:

Ventura County: *Sespe area,* one of the wildest, roughest, most intriguing areas of southern Caifornia, reached by winding roads and trails from Fillmore, Santa Paula, and Piru; before entering area, inquire about times of closure because of fire and other hazards. Recommended only for experienced hikers. A maze of narrow canyons (many with streams); chaparral and oak-covered hills and mountains. Deer, brown bears, and other mammals including cougars. California Condor Refuge not open to visitors.

Los Angeles County: *Stockton Flats Campground* (elevation 5,500 ft.), 7 miles west of Glen Ranch Resort in North Fork of Lytle Creek Canyon. Road very poor. Open all year. Water available. Follow trails to observe interesting mountain flora and fauna. A climb may reward one with sight of Bighorn Sheep.

San Diego County: *Laguna Mountains,* bordering Colorado Desert. Pine and deciduous oak forest. Steep eastern escarpment offers magnificent views of desert. U.S. Forest Service Public Camps.

Agua Caliente Springs Park, 22 miles south of Scissors Crossing turnoff on Highway 78. Regional desert park with many facilities, including electricity.

Vallecito Park, 17 miles south of Scissors Crossing turn-off on Highway 78. Regional desert park. Vallecito Stage Station historical restoration and landmark.

Palomar Mountain Park, reached by way of Stars-to-Skyline Drive. Small wilderness-type park. Gateway to interesting area of Yellow Pine, Incense Cedar, Coulter Pine, California Black Oak, Goldcup Oak. Madrone in area nearby, also Euonymous *(E. parishii),* both rare plants in southern California.

Anza-Borrego State Park, a large area of typical Colorado Desert. Mostly devoid of trees but abounding in agave, Ocotillo, and cactus. Desert Willow and Mesquite in washes, and Washingtonia Palm *(Washingtonia filifera)* in larger canyons leading westward to higher mountains. Badlands scenery, fossil and gypsum beds, eroded clay formations. Excellent interpretive trails and campfire programs.

San Bernardino County: *Holcomb Valley Campground,* 3 miles north of Big Bear Lake in San Bernardino Mountains, entered by way of Polique Canyon Road ½ mile west of Big Bear Ranger Station. Center of remarkable Piñon, Western Juniper, Yellow Pine, and Mountain Mahogany area. Birds, insects, and high mountain shrubs and trees. No water.

San Gorgonio Wild Life Area, best entered from Barton Flats. Primitive camping permitted only at designated campsites. Campfire permit required; at Mill Creek Ranger Station or Barton Falts Station. Two-pound axe with 26-inch handle, and shovel with 8-inch blade and over-all length of 36 inches required. Area leads to wilderness high-country of Upper Transition and Boreal conditions.

Riverside County: *Joshua Tree National Monument,* an area of over 850 square miles, mostly in Little San Bernardino Mountains and adjacent Mojave Desert, including parts of Coxcomb Mountains. Typical high and low desert. Joshua Tree, Washingtonia Palm, One-Leaf Piñon Pine, California Juniper, Bigelow's Cholla, Bigelow's Nolina. Bighorn Sheep. Splendid eroded granite formations and fine distant views of Colorado Desert. Nature trails and a museum. Year-round camping in specified campgrounds; water and wood not generally available. Headquarters at Twentynine Palms, California.

Painted Canyon and Box Canyon, in Mecca Mud Hills, reached by Highway 195 leading eastward from Mecca and to Desert Center. Two flat-bottomed canyons in close proximity, cut deeply into old lake-bottom clays and sandstone deposits. Vertical canyon walls highly colored and of fantastic beauty; side canyons often narrow and winding. Ironwood Tree, rare Orcutt Aster *(Aster orcuttii),* and other plants in recesses of gorges, highly heated in summer and subject to occasional torrential summer cloudbursts. No campgrounds maintained.

Inyo County: *Death Valley National Monument,* most scenic awe-inspiring region in southern California, visited by thousands every year. Spectacular mountain walls and colorful canyons. Large sunken area, with its lowest parts 282 feet below sea level. Over its nearly flat floor many good roads lead to points of interest. Several well-equipped campgrounds, and accommodations for casual visitors. Two well-appointed museums intepret its natural history. Best time of year from October 1 to January 1, but there are many pleasant calm days up to May 1, when hot season begins. Summer visitation allowed, but not advisable except in higher mountains.

Santa Barbara County: *Refugio Beach and Canyon,* on Highway 101 about 15 miles west of Goleta. Beautiful picnic area. Roadside botanizing and insect collecting on road up canyon and through Refugio Pass. Live Oak, chaparral, Madrone.

Jamala Beach off Highway 1, west of Santa Barbara. Rock collecting, fossils, beach pebbles, etc.

Davey Brown Camp, reached by Figueroa Mountain road out of Santa Inez. Fine for botanizing and observation of wildlife. At edge of Santa Inez Wilderness Area. Red Rock Camp, on upper part of Santa Inez River, off Highway 154 after you travel over San Marcos Pass. At edge of Wilderness Area.

El Capitan Beach Park on Highway 101. 20 miles west of Santa Barbara. Sandy and rocky beach. Sea life, fossil collecting, etc.

The director of Parks and Recreation of each of the southern California counties publishes a list of all parks and recreation areas in his county. The State Division of Beaches and Parks publishes a similar list for state parks. You can obtain these lists from the the county offices at the courthouse in the county seat and from the state office at Sacramento. Many of the areas listed can serve as camp headquarters for excursions by foot or automobile into adjacent scenic areas to observe the natural history. The United States Forest Service issues detailed maps showing campsites in the forests. The forest rangers supply maps and information upon request. Often they can suggest scenic trails leading to places of unusual interest.

The Secretary of the U. S. Department of the Interior has announced a far-reaching plan for conservation of wildlife, natural areas, and the recreational potential of the Lower Colorado River area. The program will be developed through the combined efforts of the Department of the Interior, three states, and numerous local communities along 265 miles of the river. Under the plan, the natural beauty of almost 400,000 acres will be dedicated to public recreational use.

NATURE TRAILS

Nature trails enable visitors to get a good general idea of an area (particularly of its flora) in a very short time. They are very helpful to beginners in nature study.

Nature trails in our state parks, botanical gardens, and arboretums lead from one numbered and labeled stake to another, with information about the names of plants, bird nests, animal tracks, and insect colonies. At the entrance to a self-guided nature trail, there is usually an explanatory pamphlet which you may borrow as you walk through. A small charge may be made if you wish to keep the printed guide. You can walk over the trails at your leisure, take valuable notes, and perhaps make some drawings or take a few close-up pictures to help you remember the wonderful things you have seen.

Santa Barbara: Santa Barbara Botanical Garden. Self-explanatory nature trail among unique trees, shrubs, ferns, flowers.

Los Angeles: U.C.L.A. Botanical Garden. Nature trail among exotic and native plants.

Claremont: Rancho Santa Ana Botanical Gardens. Native plants and plant-community plots.

Death Valley: Badwater. A 55-mile self-interpreting drive. Colorful canyons, salt pools, etc.

La Cañada: Descanso Gardens. Many unusual plants well labeled.

Mitchell's Caverns, San Bernardino County: Mary Beal Trail (named in honor of the well-known desert botanist) in newly created desert state park. Eastern Mojave Desert plants.

Twentynine Palms: Joshua Tree National Monument Headquarters. Oasis park with well-labeled nature trail, also a fine little museum where information is supplied and exhibits shown. Other nature trails in Monument: Salton View; cholla gardens in Pinto Basin; and Arch-Rock Nature Trail, consisting of posts with explanatory texts.

Palm Desert: Plants of desert-wash community in natural setting along well-labeled trail maintained by Palm Springs Desert Museum.

Anza-Borrego State Park: Borrego Palm Canyon. Another trail, in Split Mountain Canyon, is of geological interest.

MUSEUMS, ZOOS, AND BOTANICAL GARDENS

Arcadia: *Los Angeles State and County Arboretum,* 301 N. Baldwin Ave. Natural History Museum. Native and exotic trees. Daily 9 A.M. to dusk. Free.

Bloomington: *San Bernardino County Museum,* 18860 Orange St. Natural History Museum. Free. Evening Lectures. Mon.–Sun. 1–5.

China Lake, San Bernardino County: *Maturango Museum,* 7th and Orange Sts. Natural history, minerals, etc. Free.

Claremont: *Rancho Santa Ana Botanical Garden,* 1500 N. College. Native California plants. Plant communities garden. Nature trail. Mon.–Sat. 8–5.; Sun. 10–5. Free.

Death Valley: *Death Valley Museum.* Natural History Museum. Open daily Free. *Pacific Coast Borax Museum.* Open daily.

Independence: *Eastern California Museum.* Natural history. Monthly field trips. Mon.–Sat. 10–12, 1–5; Sun. 1–5. Free.

La Cañada: *Descanso Gardens,* 1418 Descanso Drive. Botanical Garden Field trips for all school grades through college. Free.

La Jolla: T. Wayland Vaughn, *Aquarium-Museum of Natural History.* Museum of Oceanic Studies and Aquarium. Mon.–Fri. 9–5; Sat., Sun., and holidays 10–6. Free.

Los Angeles: *Griffith Park, Griffith Observatory and Planetarium.* Tues.–Sun., 2–10. Planetarium: adults 60 cents, children 30 cents. *Griffith Park Zoological Garden,* containing more than a thousand animals. Botanical garden in dell. Adults 25 cents; children free. Greater Los Angeles Zoo to be a unit of vast city recreation and park systems. Present zoo then to be used as a compound for assembly and conditioning of animals in transit to new zoo, which is to be a living museum of world's fauna. Children's zoo to be much like that at San Diego. Daily 10–5.

Los Angeles: *Los Angeles County Museum,* Exposition Park. Natural history, archaeology, mineralogy, Indian lore. Tues.–Sun. 1–5. Free.

Los Angeles: *Southwest Museum.* Indian Museum, 10 Highland Park. Memorable collection of Southwestern Indian material. Tues.–Sun. 1–5. Free.

Los Angeles: *University of California Botanical Gardens,* 405 Hilgard Ave. Daily. 8–5. Free.

Palm Springs: *Palm Springs Desert Museum,* 135 E. Tahquitz Drive. Natural History Museum. Wildlife sanctuary.

Evening Programs, field trips. Oct. 15—May 31, Mon.—Sat. 10—5; Sun. 1—4.

Riverside: *Riverside Municipal Museum.* General Museum, 7th and Orange Sts. Mon.—Sat. 9—5. Classes for children, evening lectures. Free.

San Diego: *Balboa Park, San Diego Museum of Man,* Mon.— Sat. 10—4:45; Sun. 12—4:45. Free. *San Diego Zoological Garden.* One of the largest and best-administered zoos in the world, with 4,000 animals. Children's zoo especially attractive for youngsters. Daily 9—5. Adults $1.00; children under 16 free. *Natural History Museum.* Exhibits of birds, mammals, insects, marine life, plants, minerals and other resources. Open daily 10 to 4:30.

San Marino: *Harry E. Huntington Botanical Garden.* 200 acres with 50,000 plants, featuring desert plants: Cycad collection, Palm collection etc. Open 1:00—4:30 P.M. except on Monday and certain holidays. (Closed during October).

San Pedro: *Marine Museum,* near beach. Specializing in sea life. Open daily. Free.

Santa Barbara: *Santa Barbara Botanic Garden,* 1212 Mission Canyon Road. Open daily 8 A.M. to sunset. Native plants, nature trails, talks, field trips, tours, courses and research. *Santa Barbara Museum of Natural History,* 2559 Puesta Del Sol Road. Open daily 9 to 5; Sundays 1 to 5. Indian exhibits, animal and plant life, rock and mineral displays, planetarium.

Santa Maria: *Walker Grove County Park.* Small zoological garden, including aviary.

Thousand Oaks: *Conejo Canyon, Jungleland,* wild-animal ranch where animals are trained for movies. One-hour "Wild Animal Circus" given on Saturday afternoons and all day Sunday. Adults $1.; children 50 cents.

WHERE TO OBTAIN HELP

Many institutions and organizations invite participation and give information to those interesed in nature. The National Audubon Society maintains the Audubon Center of Southern California (1000 North Durfee Ave., P.O. Box 3666, El Monte, California). Natural science books, pictures, charts, pamphlets, and supplies are on sale at the Center. The society supervises a protected area (127 acres) of bottom land for observation and research, and five miles of trails. Groups must arrange in advance to be taken by a teacher-naturalist over the trails. The sanctuary is open 9 A.M. to 5 P.M., and is free to the public.

Audubon Society branches in southern California are as follows:

Buena Vista Audubon Society meets third Thursday; publishes *The Lagoon Flyer.*

Los Angeles Audubon Society meets second Tuesday; publishes *Western Tanager.*

Pasadena Audubon Society meets last Saturday; publishes *Wren-Tit.*

Pomona Valley Audubon Society meets first Thursday; publishes *Chaparral Naturalist.*

San Bernardino Audubon Society meets third Wednesday; publishes *The Western Meadowlark.*

San Diego Audubon Society meets last Saturday; publishes *Sketches.*

San Fernando Valley Audubon Society meets first Friday; publishes *The Phainopepla.*

Santa Barbara Audubon Society meet fourth Friday.

Sea and Sage Audubon Society meets third Tuesday; publishes *Wandering Tattler.*

Whittier Audubon Society meets third Tuesday; publishes *The Whittier Observer.*

Other organizations are listed below:

Cooper Ornithological Society has southern California division that usually meets in Los Angeles County Museum.

Desert Protective Council (Box 33, Banning, California), active organization of almost a thousand members seeking to protect southwestern deserts and promote appreciation of arid lands everywhere. Activities include public meetings, press releases, participation in conservation movements. and promotion of legislation protecting deserts. An educational foundation prints and distributes leaflets to teachers.

Federation of Outdoor Clubs (established in 1932) for mutual service and for proper management, enjoyment and protection of America's scenic wilderness and recreational resources. Publishes *Western Outdoor Quarterly.*

The Federation is represented in southern California by the Desmont Club (388 Dearborn Ave., Pasadena), the San Antonio Club (215 "J" South Alamansor Ave., Alhambra), and the Sierra Club (headquarters at 1056 Mills Tower, San Francisco, with local southern California chapters at Riverside, San Diego, and Los Padres).

These organizations are very active in promoting preservation of primitive areas, spots of scenic beauty and especially in mountaineering. Chapters have monthly meetings and conduct many field trips.

Southern California Botanists, a group of professional and amateur botanists meeting several times a year to conduct trips to gardens, forests, and deserts, and visits to botanical research institutions.

The Wilderness Society (head office at 2184 "P" St. N.W., Washington, D. C.), aims to secure preservation of wilderness through an educational program to mobilize public cooperation in resisting invasion of wilderness. Publishes *The Living Wilderness.*

California Garden Clubs, Inc. (340 S. San Pedro St., Los Angeles 15). Chief interests beautiful gardens, conservation and preservation of California landscape. Discussions and garden trips. Local clubs in many cities and towns. Publishes *Golden Gardens.*

Defenders of Wildlife (809 Dupont Circel Building, Washington, D. C.). Promotes humane education and dissemination of knowledge concerning life history and ecology of fur-bearers. Publishes a quarterly news bulletin *Defenders of Wildlife,* and many pamphlets for teachers and students.

Conchological Club of Southern California meets in Los Angeles County Museum first Monday at 7:30 P.M.

Pacific Shell Club meets third Sunday, September through May at 2 P.M. in the Los Angeles County Museum.

San Diego Shell Club meets second Thursday at 7:30 P.M. at San Diego Museum of Natural History.

Yucaipa Shell Club meets third Sunday at 2:30 P.M. at Museum of Natural History of Yucaipa.

SUPPLIES AND EQUIPMENT

Supplies and equipment for nature study can be purchased from College Biological Supply Co., P.O. Box 1326, Escondido, California; General Biological Supply House, Inc., 8200 South Hoyne Ave., Chicago, Illinois; Bio-Metal Associates, Box 61, Santa Monica, California 90401; Clo Wind, 827 Congress Ave., Pacific Grove, California 93942; Ward's of California, P.O. Box 1749, Monterey, California 93942.

SUGGESTED REFERENCES

Abrams, Leroy. *Illustrated Flora of the Pacific States*. Stanford: Stanford University Press, 1959. 4 vols.

*Benson, Lyman, and Robert Darrow. *A Manual of Southwestern Trees and Shrubs*. Tucson: University of Arizona, 1945.

Burt, Wiliam H., and Richard P. Grossenheider. *A Field Guide to the Mammals*. Boston: Houghton Mifflin Co., 1952.

Cahalane, Victor H. *Mammals or North America*. New York: Macmillan Co., 1947.

*Comstock, John H. *The Spider Book*. Ithaca: Comstock Publishing Co., 1948.

Durrenberger, R. W. *The Geography of California*. Los Angeles: Brewster Publications, 1959.

*Essig, Edward O. *Insects and Mites of Western North America*. New York: The Macmillan Co., 1958.

Gertsch, Willis J. *American Spiders*. Princeton: Van Nostrand, 1949.

*Grinnell, Joseph. *The Biota of the San Bernardino Mountains*. Univ. Calif. Publ. Zool. Vol. 5, No. 1. Berkeley: University of California Press, 1908.

*Grinnell, Joseph, and H. S. Swarth. *An Account of the Birds and Mammals of the San Jacinto Area of Southern California*. Univ. Calif. Publ. Zool. Vol. 10, No. 10. Berkeley: University of California Press, 1913.

Hoffman, Ralph. *Birds of the Pacific States*. Boston: Houghton Mifflin Co., 1927.

Ingles, Lloyd G. *Mammals of the Pacific States*. Stanford: Stanford University Press, 1965.

Jaeger, Edmund C. *The California Deserts*. Stanford: Stanford University Press, 1965.
Desert Wild Flowers. Stanford: Stanford University Press,
Desert Wildlife. Stanford: Stanford University Press, 1961.
A Naturalist's Death Valley. Palm Desert: Desert Magazine Press, 1957.

Jepson, Willis L. *A Manual of the Flowering Plants of California*. Berkeley: University of California Press, 1957.

*Out of print. Consult your local library.

[100]

Kirk, Ruth. *Exploring Death Valley*. Stanford: Stanford University Press, 1965.

McMinn, Howard E. *An Illustrated Manual of California Shrubs*. Berkeley and Los Angeles: University of California Press, 1959.

Morris, Percy A. *A Field Guide to the Shells of the Pacific Coast and Hawaii*. Boston: Houghton Mifflin Co., 1952.

Munz, Philip A. *California Desert Wildflowers*. Berkeley and Los Angeles: University of California Press, 1962.

A California Flora. Berkeley and Los Angeles: University of California Press, 1961.

California Spring Wildflowers. Berkeley and Los Angeles: University of California Press, 1961.

California Mountain Wildflowers. Berkeley and Los Angeles: University of California Press, 1963.

Murie, Olaus. *A Field Guide to Animal Tracks*. Boston: Houghton Mifflin Co., 1954.

Pequegnat, Willis E. *The Biota of the Santa Ana Mountains*. Jour. Entomol. and Zool., Vol. 42, Nos. 4 and 4. Claremont, 1951.

Peterson, Roger Tory. *A Field Guide to Western Birds*. Boston: Houghton Mifflin Co., 1960.

Pough, Frederick H. *A Field Guide to Rocks and Minerals*. Boston: Houghton Mifflin Co., 1953.

Ricketts, Edward F., and Jack Calvin. Rev. by Joel W. Hedgpeth. *Between Pacific Tides*. 3rd Ed. Stanford: Stanford University Pres, 1962.

Stebbins, Robert C. *Amphibians and Reptiles of Western North America*. New York: McGraw-Hill, 1954.

Usinger, Robert L. *Aquatic Insects of California*. Berkeley: University of California Press, 1956.

INDEX

207407

UE